D A V I D   H A W K I N S

EDITOR

# A TEAM-BASED LEARNING GUIDE FOR FACULTY

## *in the*

# HEALTH PROFESSIONS

authorHOUSE®

*AuthorHouse™ LLC*
*1663 Liberty Drive*
*Bloomington, IN 47403*
*www.authorhouse.com*
*Phone: 1-800-839-8640*

*Published by AuthorHouse 07/26/2014*

*ISBN: 978-1-4969-2929-7 (sc)*
*ISBN: 978-1-4969-2928-0 (e)*

# DEDICATION

We dedicate this book to Dr. Larry Michaelsen, the inventor of Team-Based Learning (TBL). Dr. Michaelsen invented TBL while teaching a course in management to a large class at the University of Oklahoma. Dr. Michaelsen is known and respected all around the world for his teaching and innovation in education. He has given countless workshops and seminars on TBL, has been the author and editor of four books on TBL, and has been enormously helpful to numerous faculty whose passion is to engage students in active learning, critical thinking, and problem solving.

Even though TBL got its start in the field of business at the University of Oklahoma, it is now being used in over 80 academic disciplines at more than 200 universities throughout the world. Among other disciplines, TBL has become a very prominent pedagogical strategy for teaching and learning in the health sciences. As far as we know, the first academic program to design its entire curriculum on a TBL frame is the College of Pharmacy at California Northstate University in Sacramento. Many other pharmacy schools have incorporated TBL into their curriculum and numerous other schools in medicine, nursing, and allied health have adopted TBL as the preferred method of converting courses to an active learning format.

In his 39 years of academic life, Dr. Michaelsen has received numerous awards for his outstanding teaching and for his pioneering work in TBL. The authors of this book will always remember him for the help and inspiration he gave us as we began the tedious but intellectually stimulating process of transforming pharmacy education into an active learning pedagogy.

# CONTRIBUTORS

David Hawkins, PharmD
Vice President for Academic Affairs and
Founding Dean of Pharmacy
California Health Sciences University

Robert Clegg, PhD
Associate Professor of Administrative Sciences
California Health Sciences University

Grant D. Lackey, PharmD
Associate Dean for Experiential Education
Associate Professor of Clinical Sciences
California Health Sciences University

John R. Martin, PhD
Associate Dean for Academic Affairs and Assessment
Professor of Pharmacology
California Health Sciences University

Dean X. Parmelee, MD
Associate Dean for Academic Affairs
Boonshoft School of Medicine
Wright State University

Rajat Sethi, PhD
Chair of Pharmaceutical and Biomedical Sciences
Associate Professor of Pharmacology
California Health Sciences University

# TABLE OF CONTENTS

# FOREWORD

## *Dean X. Parmelee, MD*

Teaching in the health professions has many rewards, the greatest one being that, if we do a good job, our learners can become good practitioners in the healing arts and lead lives of service. It's the doing the 'good job' that this book is all about.

Higher education is undergoing a healthy transformation driven by the burgeoning global economy, technology, generational shifts, and a political and fiscal demand for greater accountability. Health professions education is not spared by these influences and has the additional one of improving the efficiency of health care delivery with increased patient safety and continuous quality improvement. Competency-based education and training has become the guiding force for curricula in the health professions.

*A Team-Based Learning Guide for Faculty in the Health Professions*, authored by faculty at California Health Sciences University represents an innovative and courageous work to create a new professional curriculum using Team-Based Learning™(TBL) as its principal instructional strategy. They started this endeavor with the premise that their learners could become better practitioners if their curriculum demanded active and engaged learning, the kind of learning that lasts and becomes the habit of life-long learning. Every course they designed started with the question: "What do we want our students to be able to do when they have finished this course?" Most of the chapters in the book present a course or topic area and start with this question – which leads to the student learning outcomes (SLO), taking the reader through the steps and details of how to build a learning module with TBL.

Three more questions frame each chapter: "What does the student need to know to be able to do ___?" "How do we facilitate their learning?" and "How do we assess what they have learned?" At its heart, TBL is the strategy for addressing these fundamental pedagogical queries and generating solid learning outcomes. The SLOs are translated graphically in each chapter into a competency rubric that provides learner and instructor with benchmarks on progress. What is especially nice about the competency rubric is that it is in a 'Milestones'- ready format that medical residencies and medical schools are adopting.

This *Guide* is perfect for the health professions educator who wants to do 'something' in the classroom that truly engages the learners with the material and have what they learn last beyond the term of the course. To be successful with TBL is a great deal of work – much harder than putting together a few hours of lecture notes and PowerPoints – and it requires learning about learner-centered education. In the *Guide*, you will find good examples of *Individual Readiness Assurance* questions, detailed examples of *Application Exercises*, resource listings for the students that are annotated for clarifying what's most important, grading schemas that tie together the assessment process. In addition, the editor, David Hawkins, has written the first chapter to explain why they feel TBL is the best strategy for health professions students and the concluding chapter on how faculty and its leadership can create a 'culture' that sustains TBL and makes it more vibrant. Working with this book can help you build a new and successful course with TBL.

# PREFACE

## *David Hawkins, Pharm D.*

"Why is it, in spite of the fact that teaching by pouring in, learning by passive absorption, are universally condemned, that they are still so entrenched in practice?" (John Dewey, *Democracy in Education*, 1916, page 46)

The purpose of this book is to provide a concise instructor's guide on how to transform a boring, passive learning pedagogy into a vibrant, active learning environment. We have known for more than a hundred years that lecturing to students leads to bulimic learning. Students are able to memorize lecture notes, regurgitate what they have memorized on an exam, pass the exam, but then soon forget most of what they memorized. This type of learning is shallow and ineffective and should be condemned by all instructors. And, yet, it is still as prevalent in the hallowed lecture halls today as it was back in the time of John Dewey. Let's be honest. During a lecture many students spend their time texting friends, visiting Facebook, checking emails, daydreaming, or even snoozing. They are not engaged, and why should they be? They have copies of their instructor's power point slides and may even have access to the audio- or video-taped lecture. In fact, they may not even come to class, but rather subscribe to student-generated lecture notes and spend their valuable time sleeping, shopping, exercising, or going to a movie for some real entertainment.

Timeliness

It is time for curriculum reform. And, it is beginning to take place in medical schools, pharmacy schools, and in many other disciplines. But there is always resistance to change. Faculty enjoy being the " sage on the stage," and it is relatively easy to create a lecture, especially with the aid of numerous "power pointless" slides to keep the instructor on track, even if he or she is the only one riding the train.

One of the driving forces behind incorporating active learning strategies in health sciences curricula is that programmatic accreditation agencies now require it. For the past several years, medical schools have met the requirement by introducing problem-based learning (PBL) into the curriculum. They did this by converting a single course or a portion of a course into a PBL format. A few medical schools actually converted all didactic courses into PBL modules. Now we are seeing more and more medical schools converting from PBL to team-based learning (TBL) because the faculty has come to understand that TBL requires fewer faculty resources and the learning is faculty directed rather than student driven.

Some of the authors of this book took a bold step several years ago and decided to design an entire pharmacy school didactic curriculum on a team-based, active learning frame. What made this decision less painful and difficult to make than usual was the fact that we were starting a new college of pharmacy, and so we were starting from scratch. We invited several experts to give TBL faculty workshops at our school and we provided close mentoring to newly hired faculty. Over the course of four years, we completed our task of creating all required and elective course offerings in the TBL format recommended by the inventor of TBL, Dr. Larry Michaelsen. In the final chapter of this book we share some of the lessons learned and changes we made as we continued developing our curriculum.

If you are committed to enhancing student learning then you will abandon the lecture that leads to passive learning and create ways to engage students into active learning. When it comes to health professions education, we think TBL is the best method for maintaining an active learning environment that stimulates thinking and makes learning passionate, relevant, and fun.

Scope

The authors of this book represent different disciplines taught in health professional schools. Each author has employed the backward design explained in the first chapter to discuss the four steps for designing a TBL unit of instruction, namely:

1. Defining learning outcomes and developing application exercises;
2. Determining what fundamental concepts need to be learned and writing learning objectives for those concepts;
3. Designing guided learning materials that are used during pre-class independent study to facilitate student learning; and
4. Developing both formative and summative tools for assessing learning outcomes.

The topics covered in this book represent a wide range of subjects including anatomy and physiology, pathophysiology, pharmacology, toxicology, clinical therapeutics, geriatrics, biostatistics, clinical epidemiology, and evidence-based medicine. What we hope the reader will realize is that regardless of the subject matter, any topic can be developed and delivered using a TBL approach.

The unique aspect of our book is the attention we give to defining learning outcomes and developing both formative and summative assessments of student learning (Steps 1 and 4 of the Backward Design Approach). Assessment of student learning has become a major criterion for obtaining and sustaining regional accreditation of all colleges and universities in the United States. And, well it should be. How do you know if students are learning what you want them to learn? Course exams provide some data, but as already mentioned the learning that leads to a passing grade on exams may be very shallow and associated with a low retention rate. It is only when students are actively engaged in learning that knowledge is actually constructed in their minds, and when they apply that knowledge repetitively in solving relevant problems, the learning becomes deep and the retention of knowledge is enhanced. The authors of this book illustrate how one should go about defining a set of learning outcomes for a wide range of topics and how to design simple instruments that can be used to assess those outcomes.

In our experience, formative assessments of learning are best carried out using multiple choice exams. Depending on the phase of learning, we assess student learning using RATS, BATS, and CATS. The RATS are Readiness Assurance Tests and give students feedback on how well they have grasped and learned fundamental course concepts. This also serves as an indicator to how prepared they are for applying what they have learned. The BATS are Basic Application Tasks that inform students on the progress being made in accomplishing course learning outcomes. And, CATS are Cumulative Assessment Tests that are used to measure knowledge retention and the integration of new knowledge with what has already been learned.

The key to summative learning assessments is to focus on a few salient course learning outcomes that can be measured using a tool with which there is high inter-rater reliability. We have found that a carefully constructed rubric is the best assessment tool.

Just think if you follow the guide we have put together for faculty in the health professions, you can convert the course or topics that you teach into a dynamic laboratory in which teaching facilitates learning and learning is actively absorbed and assessed.

# CHAPTER 1

# Rationale and Method for Developing Team-Based Learning Education
## *David Hawkins, Pharm D.*

Team-Based Learning (TBL) is a well-defined active learning strategy that combines pre-class guided self-learning with highly interactive small group learning in class. It has a great advantage over other small group methods, such as problem-based learning, because multiple teams can be facilitated by a single faculty facilitator rather than multiple facilitators, and the learning is faculty-directed. TBL emphasizes the importance of individual accountability, team-work, and the application of basic, fundamental concepts in solving real world problems. The role of the instructor is to clearly articulate the learning outcomes, create challenging problems for students to solve, and probe their reasoning in reaching conclusions.

Designing team-based learning instruction does require more time and effort than the traditional lecture-based, passive learning style of teaching, but it is well worth the extra time and effort. Several published studies have documented the benefits of TBL including enhancing clinical problem solving (Bick et al; Beatty et al), having a positive impact on student engagement and learning satisfaction, (Chung et al; Clark et al), improving student performance (Zgheib et al; Vasan et al; Thomas et al; Tan N, et al), and sharpening critical thinking skills and long-term retention (McInerney and Fink).

The format for TBL is comprised of three phases as shown in the diagram below.

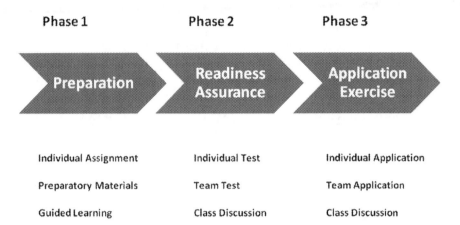

| Phase 1 | Phase 2 | Phase 3 |
| --- | --- | --- |
| **Preparation** | **Readiness Assurance** | **Application Exercise** |
| Individual Assignment | Individual Test | Individual Application |
| Preparatory Materials | Team Test | Team Application |
| Guided Learning | Class Discussion | Class Discussion |

**Adapted from: Michaelsen LK et al. Team-Based Learning for Health Professions Education**

In Phase 1, learners study independently outside of class using guided learning materials to master course objectives and fundamental concepts. This may involve audio-taped mini-lectures, reading assignments, or other activities. In Phase 2, individual learners complete a multiple choice exam to assure their readiness to apply the concepts learned during Phase 1. This is referred to as the Individual Readiness Assurance Test (IRAT). Then the same multiple choice test is given to each team which must reach a consensus on the answer for each question. This is referred to as the Team Readiness Assurance Test (TRAT). Written appeals may be submitted by any team who would like to challenge the instructor on the correct answer or the adequacy of Phase 1 assignments. Appeals that are upheld are rewarded by giving extra grade points to the team that made the appeal. After the TRAT, the instructor provides immediate feedback on the concepts covered on the test by engaging the students in a Socratic discussion designed to clarify concepts and enhance further learning. In Phase 3, teams will complete in-class assignments that promote collaboration, use of Phase 1 and Phase 2 knowledge, and critical thinking. Again, a Socratic discussion period follows the application exercise to reinforce what was learned and to practice applying fundamental concepts to solve additional problems.

Prior to getting started with these three learning phases, the instructor will form teams comprised of 5 to 6 students based on various criteria that help achieve an even distribution of demographics, talents, and experiences across all teams. Some of the criteria used in team formation include gender, ethnicity, previous academic experience in related courses, and course-related life experiences. It is important to make the team formation process transparent and avoid using student-selected teams. Students usually remain with the same team throughout the semester for each course. All students are accountable for their own work and their team work.

A good systematic way of developing TBL instructional units is to use what is commonly referred to as the backward design approach – you begin with the end in mind and you end with knowing if you got where you intended to go. Answers to the following questions will provide a roadmap for creating an effective TBL unit, a complete course, or an entire curriculum.

1. **What do you want your students to be able to do when they have finished the course or course topic?**

The answer to this question will guide you in establishing student learning outcomes (SLOs) for the course. Once the course learning outcomes have been identified, the instructor can design the course so that students first learn fundamental course concepts and then apply those concepts to analyzing, evaluating, and synthesizing solutions to problems. The applications may involve decision-making, critical appraisal of the literature, or team projects in which the outcome sheds light on new knowledge or uses existing knowledge to solve real world problems. Creating relevant and interesting applications will not only help you organize your TBL course, but will also help you design the criteria for assessing student learning. In well-designed TBL units, the number of student learning outcomes should be in the range of three to six.

## 2. What will your students need to know in order to be able to do those things?

The answer to this question identifies the body of knowledge that must be acquired in order for students to successfully complete the application exercise mentioned in Step 1. The key to this step is identifying the fundamental course concepts that should be learned and then defining the learning objectives that must be met to learn the concepts.

Fundamental concepts are the basic units of knowledge upon which in-depth learning is constructed. Once the concepts have been identified, a set of specific learning objectives can be written that if accomplish will enable a student to grasp and understand fundamental concepts. There are usually 1 to 3 learning objectives for each fundamental concept.

## 3. How do you facilitate student learning?

TBL is inherently designed to facilitate active learning. The first phase of learning occurs during pre-class self-study, or the preparation phase. The best way to facilitate learning at this level is to provide students with a guided learning handout. Guided learning should focus on required reading assignments, mastering course concepts, accomplishing the learning objectives mentioned in Step 2, and answering probing questions integrated throughout the guided learning handout. Probing questions should engage critical thinking and stimulate deep learning (not "how should the patient be treated" but why would treatment A be preferred over treatment B for this patient?").

## 4. How do you assess student learning?

TBL lends itself well to assessing student learning objectively and on a regular basis. There are assurance tests that are designed to measure how well a student has mastered fundamental course concepts through the independent guided learning phase (pre-class self-study). As mentioned earlier, these are called **Readiness Assurance Tests (RATS)** and are administered at the beginning of a new course topic. These tests are first taken by each individual student **(IRATS)**. The exact same test is then taken by each team *(TRATS)*. During the TRAT the students engage in very rich, intellectually stimulating discussions. This is where active learning takes place as students teach each other what they need to know before going on to the application exercise. Obviously TRAT scores are almost always higher than individual scores since six heads are better than one.

## Class Discussion

After the IRAT and TRAT are both completed, time is spent in class discussing concepts that may be confusing or not sufficiently grasped from the preparation assignment before moving on to the first application exercise. The discussion time can also be used to increase the knowledge base of students by expounding and elaborating on fundamental concepts. This phase should be reasonably brief (typically less than 20 minutes) to avoid crowding out the TBL application and active learning components and to maintain student attention.

## Assessing Applications

Student learning is also assessed after application exercises have been completed. We call these assessments ***Basic Application Tasks (BATS)***. In some cases, each student will complete a portion or an abbreviated application task (***IBATS***) before working with his or her team on the full application *(TBATS)*. The assessment can be performed using an exam to determine knowledge efficiency or a rubric to measure the extent to which learning was demonstrated.

## Use of Evaluation Rubrics

A major benefit for faculty teaching outcomes-based courses is that detailed rubrics and other pertinent assessment tools make grading easier and less time consuming. There are also fewer "gray" areas because the notion of what constitutes an "A," "B," or "C" level of performance is clearly defined for faculty and students alike. Knowing specifically what constitutes the criteria for students' achievement of a certain performance level makes grading more a matter of checking content and criteria than it does creating or re-explaining that criteria. Once the initial work has been completed upfront of creating meaningful, effective assessment tools, the hardest part of grading has been accomplished. Faculty must naturally revisit the assessments to ensure that they accurately gauge student learning and must make adjustments based on SLOs, but this work pays off in improved SLOs, easier grading down the line, and improved student engagement. Because students know what the expectations are for their learning, they tend to have more positive learning and evaluation experiences and they know exactly where they stand in their courses and why. Students then become focused on their own outcomes' achievement, and this focused effort leads to a higher quality of learning and an awareness of the SLOs. In addition, when using a rubric, there are no inflated or distorted grades based on the practices of recognizing student effort, grading on a curve, or awarding extra credit.

## How to Create Evaluation Rubrics

### Step One:

Once Student Learning Outcomes have been identified, descriptors for several levels of student performance can be determined and developed. These descriptors, called indicators or criteria, describe the knowledge, skills, attitudes and/or understanding that a student needs to demonstrate at each performance level. Answers to the following questions will help in the identification and development of indicators:

- What behaviors should a student exhibit to demonstrate that he or she has achieved the expected outcome?
- What elements of a student's work would show that he or she has achieved the expected outcome?
- What does a student need to demonstrate to show that he or she "gets it"?

- What should a student do and say to demonstrate that his or her knowledge, attitudes, beliefs and motivation has attained a high level of development?

## Step Two:

The second step involves defining levels of performance and achievement, and then creating descriptors to be used to measure achievement of each level of performance. Thus, one needs to establish what each performance level looks like so that the descriptor for each level clearly defines what a student needs to demonstrate to attain each level of development. Consider the following:

- What does an "A," or "Proficient," level of performance look like? What are all the elements that need to be demonstrated by a student at the highest level of performance? What can a student at the "Proficient" level demonstrate? How does one know that this level has been achieved? What criteria need to be met for a student to demonstrate he or she has achieved this level?
- What does a "B," or "Developed," level of performance look like? How is it similar to the "A" level? How does it differ? What would a student at this level need to demonstrate in order to attain the next highest level of achievement; that is, what is it that a student at this level cannot demonstrate that a student at the highest level of achievement can demonstrate?
- What does a "C," or "Developing," level of performance look like? What differentiates it from the "B" level? What knowledge or understanding is a student at this level lacking that prevents him or her from performing at the next highest level?
- What does "D," or "Initial", level of performance look like? What is it that a student cannot demonstrate that prevents him or her from performing at the next highest level? What does the "Initial" level of performance look like? How does an evaluator know the performance level is "Initial"?
- Once a rubric has been created, use it to determine if it easily allows you, as the evaluator, to rate a student's performance. Determine

if anything is missing and then add the missing element to the rubric. Determine if you are having trouble choosing between two performance levels as this is where the rubric needs additional information or more detail.

An example of a rubric for evaluating student learning is shown in the table below.

| Indicators | Initial | Developing | Developed | Proficient |
| --- | --- | --- | --- | --- |
| Describes the pathophysiological mechanism of type 1 and type 2 diabetes. | Is unable to demonstrate an understanding of the physiology and pathophysiology of both types of diabetes. | Demonstrates a rudimentary understanding that lacks detailed information of the physiology and pathophysiology of diabetes. | Demonstrates a complete understanding of the physiology and pathophysiology of diabetes, but cannot fully integrate the effect of diabetes on all organ systems. | Demonstrates a complete understanding of the physiology and pathophysiology and can fully integrate the pathophysiological changes in all organ systems. |
| Identifies potential targets based on the major classes of medications used to treat both types of diabetes. | Is unable to identify diabetic medications based on major classes and cannot demonstrate an understanding of the targets of medications or their mechanisms of action. | Identifies a few diabetic medications based on major classes and demonstrates a rudimentary understanding of the targets of medications and their mechanisms of action. | Identifies most diabetic medications based on major classes and demonstrates an understanding of the targets of the medications and their mechanisms of action. | Identifies all diabetic medications based on major classes and demonstrates a complete understanding of the targets of the medications and their mechanisms of action. |

| | | | | |
|---|---|---|---|---|
| Describes the main therapeutic and adverse effects of medications used to treat diabetes and is able to select alternative agents to minimize adverse effects. | Is unable to demonstrate an understanding of how medications affect the diabetic patient including their beneficial and harmful effects, and is unable to select alternative agents that would minimize adverse effects. | Can describe how a few of the medications used to treat diabetes affect the diabetic patient including their beneficial and harmful effects, and has difficulty selecting alternative agents that would minimize adverse effects. | Can describe how most of the medications used to treat diabetes affect the diabetic patient including their beneficial and harmful effects, and can select some alternative agents that would minimize adverse effects. | Can describe how all of the medications used for the treatment of diabetes affect the diabetic patient including the beneficial and harmful effects of these agents, and can select all of the alternative medications that would minimize the adverse effects. |
| Demonstrates the ability to design patient-specific treatment regimens. | Is unable to design patient-specific treatment plans. | Displays a rudimentary ability to design patient-specific treatment plans. | Is able to design patient-specific treatment plans but cannot develop alternative plans. | Designs well-developed patient-specific treatment plans as well as well thought out alternative plans. |

## References

Bick RJ, Oakes JL, Actor JK, et al. Integrative Teaching: Problem Solving and Integration of Basic Science Concepts into Clinical Scenarios using Team-Based Learning. J Int Assoc Med Sci Ed 2009; 19 – 1:26-34.

Beatty S, Kelley K, Metzger A, et al. Team-based learning in therapeutics workshop sessions. Am J Pharm Ed 2009; 73:1-7.

Chung E-K, Rhee J-A, Baik Y-H, et al. The effect of team-based learning in medical ethics education. Med Teacher 2009; 31:1013-1017.

Clark MC, Nguyen HT, Bray C, et al. Team-based learning in an undergraduate nursing course. J Nurs Educ 2008; 47:111-117.

Zgheib NK, Simaan JA, Sabra R. Using team-based learning to teach pharmacology to second year medical students improves student performance. Med Teacher 2010; 32:130-135.

Vasan NS, DeFouw DO, Holland BK. Modiied use of team-based learning for effective delivery of medical gross anatomy and embryology. Anat Sci Educ 2008; 1:3-9.

Thomas PA, Bowen CW. A controlled trial of team-based learning in an ambulatory medicine clerkship for medical students. Teaching and Learning in Medicine 2011; 23:31-36.

Tan N CK, Kandiah N, Chan Y H, et al. A controlled study of team-based learning for undergraduate clinical neurology education. BMC Med Educ 2011; 11:91.

McInerney MJ, Fink D. Team-based learning enhances long-term retention and critical thinking in an undergraduate microbial physiology course. Microbiology Educ 2003; 4:3-12.

## Annotated Bibliography

*Team-Based Learning for Health Professions Education*, Larry K. Michaelsen, Dean X. Parmelee, Kathyrn K. McMahon, and Ruth E. Levine, Stylus, 2008

This book describes in detail the principles and practices of team-based learning, presents the pedagogical rationale for engaging students in active team learning instead of lecturing to students, and provides examples of the use of TBL in different heath professional disciplines.

# CHAPTER 2

# Anatomy and Physiology
## *John R. Martin, Ph D*

In this chapter, the backward design model is used to create a TBL unit in the course that covers the anatomy and physiology of the kidney. For a student to fully understand renal physiology, he or she must understand the anatomical relationships between the various segments of the nephron and the blood vessels of this system. This knowledge base is necessary in order to understand how the nephron functions in forming urine and how this contributes to the regulation of body water, electrolytes, and acid-base balance. This knowledge is also necessary for understanding the pathophysiology of renal disorders and the pharmacology of the medications that act within the tubules of the nephron. The integration of anatomy and physiology forms the foundation for understanding the pathophysiology of a variety of disorders, and the concepts involved in the diagnostic evaluation and therapeutic management of patients with these disorders.

In keeping with the backward design of courses and topics, the following description of the development of a course topic on the nephron will address, in order, the development of learning outcomes (including the development of a case study or application exercise), specific learning objectives, guided learning materials, and assessments of student learning.

1. **What do you want your students to be able to do when they have finished the course or course topic?**

When students finish this course they should be able to accomplish the following course learning outcomes:

1. Describe and discuss the anatomy and physiology of the kidney;

2. Explain the etiology and pathophysiology of the kidney disorders; and

3. Describe the mechanisms of action and the adverse effects of the medications used to treat the kidney disorders.

The learning outcomes for a course topic should align with the course learning outcomes. The learning outcomes on the anatomy and physiology of the nephron are as follows:

1. Describe and discuss the anatomy and physiology of the nephron;

2. Explain the etiology and pathophysiology of the disorders of the nephron; and

3. Describe the mechanisms of action and the adverse effects of the medications used to treat kidney disorders that affect the nephron.

**Application:**

The following is an example of an application exercise for this unit of instruction.

J. R. and his fishing buddy, J. W., become stranded on the Pacific Ocean while deep sea fishing when their boat develops engine trouble and quits. The battery also loses power and they do not have a back-up. Without a battery they cannot restart the engine or use the radio to call for help. Furthermore, since they wanted to get away from civilization, they left their cell phones at home. J. R. and J. W. are without food and little water (enough to last a couple of hours).

1. At the end of four days of waiting for help to arrive, what do you expect to have happened to the glomerular filtration rate (GFR) of J. R. and J. W.? The GRF would have

   A. **Decreased when compared to GFR from four days earlier.**
   B. Increased when compared to GFR from four days earlier.
   C. Remained the same compared to GFR from four days earlier.

2. The change in GFR that occurred in J. R. and J. W. would most likely be due to

   A. Decreased oncotic colloidal pressure.
   B. No change in oncotic colloidal pressure.
   C. **Increased oncotic colloidal pressure.**
   D. Increased synthesis of albumin in the liver.
   E. Increased synthesis and release of red blood cells into the blood.

3. The change in flow rate of the filtrate through the proximal convoluted tubule would

   A. Increase the absorption of sodium while decreasing that of water.
   B. Decrease the absorption of sodium while increasing that of water.
   C. Result in no change in sodium or water absorption.
   D. **Increase the absorption of both sodium and water.**
   E. Decrease the absorption of both sodium and water.

4. Over the four days stranded at sea, the blood levels of ADH in J. R. and J. W. would

   A. Not change.
   B. Decrease.
   C. **Increase.**

5. Changes in blood levels of ADH are generally mediated by

   I. Osmoreceptors located in the hypothalamus.
   II. Volume receptors located in the right atrium.
   III. Sodium sensing receptors in the juxtaglomeular apparatus.

   A. I only.
   B. **I and II.**
   C. I and III.

     D. II and III.

     E. I, II and III.

6. The mechanism of action of ADH on the nephron includes

    I. Stimulating the opening of aqueous pores in the luminal membrane of the epithelial cells of the collecting ducts.

    II. Stimulating renin release from the juxtaglomerular apparatus.

    III. Stimulating the activity of the $Na^+$ / $K^+$-ATPase pump in the basolateral membrane of the epithelial cells of the thick ascending Loop of Henle.

     A. I only.

     B. I and II.

     C. **I and III.**

     D. II and III.

     E. I, II and III.

7. Over the four days stranded at sea, the blood levels of aldosterone in J. R. and J. W. would

     A. decrease.

     B. **increase.**

     C. not change.

8. Changes in blood levels of aldosterone can be caused by

    I. An increase in sympathetic activity.

    II. A decrease in blood volume.

    III. An increase in blood levels of renin.

     A. I only.

     B. I and II.

     C. I and III.

     D. II and III.

     E. **I, II and III.**

9.  The reabsorption of water from the nephrons of the kidney is critically dependent on the

    I.   Cortical to medullary osmotic gradient established by the countercurrent multiplier mechanism of the loop of Henle.
    II.  Maintenance of the cortical medullary osmotic gradient by the countercurrent exchange mechanism of the vasa recta.
    III. Cortical collecting ducts being freely permeable to urea.

    A.  I only.
    B.  **I and II.**
    C.  I and III.
    D.  II and III.
    E.  I, II and III.

10. J. R. suggests to J. W. that they drink the sea water. J. W.'s response to J. R. should be

    A.  "Yes. It will alleviate our thirst."
    B.  "Yes. Sea water is hypotonic so it will replace lost water to elevate our blood volume."
    C.  "Yes. Sea water is isotonic so it will replace lost water to elevate our blood volume without affecting electrolyte balance."
    D.  "No. Sea water is hypotonic so it will further dehydrate the cells of our bodies."
    E.  **"No. Sea water is hypertonic so it will increase the osmolarity of our extracellular and intracellular fluid spaces."**

The questions listed above could be presented to individual students first (IBAT) and then to each team (TBAT). For the TBAT, the teams will simultaneously report their answer to each question. The instructor will call on a team to defend its answer and then ask other teams with different answers to present their argument for choosing an alternative answer. This will engage the class in debate. The instructor will then discuss with the class their reasoning and help the class think through the arguments to reach the right answer to the question.

## 2. What will your students need to know in order to be able to do those things?

Students will need to learn the fundamental concepts of the anatomy and physiology of the nephron in order to accomplish the learning outcomes listed under Step 1. The following learning objectives will help students grasp and understand the concepts.

The student must be able to:

1. List the segments of the nephron in the order that fluid moves through the nephron from the glomerulus to the collecting ducts.
2. Describe how pressures are regulated in the afferent and efferent arterioles to control pressures in the glomerular capillaries and how this influences the formation of filtrate.
3. Describe how each segment of the nephron handles water, $Na^+$, $K^+$, and $Cl^-$, and how this contributes to the composition of the final urine.
4. Describe the countercurrent multiplier, where it is found in the nephron and why it is important to forming concentrated or dilute urine.
5. Describe the countercurrent exchanger, where it is located and why it is important to forming concentrated urine.
6. Describe the role that antidiuretic hormone (ADH/vasopressin) plays in the formation of a concentrated urine, including the specific segments that ADH influences.
7. Describe the role of urea in the cortical to medullary osmotic gradient and how this contributes to the ability of the nephron to concentrate the forming urine.
8. Describe the role that aldosterone plays in regulating the composition of the final urine.
9. Describe the processes that occur in the collecting duct with respect to the handling of $Na^+$, $K^+$, and $H^+$.

10. List the segments of the nephron that handle $H^+$ and/or $HCO_3^-$ and describe how the management of these ions in these segments contributes to acid-base regulation.

## 3. How do you facilitate student learning?

Students need to understand how the nephron forms and concentrates urine, which means they must understand the anatomical segments of the nephron and how each segment of the nephron handles the main electrolytes ($Na^+$, $K^+$, and $Cl^-$) and water. To do this the student must understand the concepts of the countercurrent multiplier and countercurrent exchange systems and the involvement of vasopressin (or antidiuretic hormone) in the formation of concentrated urine. An understanding of these mechanisms is essential for an understanding of the effects of pharmacological agents on the function of the nephron and the formation of the final urine. The student can then apply this understanding to the pharmacotherapy of disorders (presented in a later course) that involve changes in renal function.

A guided learning handout can be provided to focus the learning on those aspects that must be learned in order to grasp and understand the fundamental concepts. The following questions can be used to guide student learning.

1. What regulates the formation of filtrate and the factors that influence its formation?
2. What segments within the nephron affect the reabsorption and secretion of $Na^+$, $K^+$, $Cl^-$, and $H_2O$ and what is the mechanism by which the reabsorption or secretion occurs?
3. What effect does aldosterone have on $Na^+$ reabsorption and where in the nephron does this take place?
4. How does ADH (vasopressin) affect $H_2O$ reabsorption and where does this occur?
5. What is the osmolarity of the filtrate at the beginning and end of each segment of the nephron and what are the mechanisms that cause these changes?

6. How does the countercurrent multiplier establish the cortical to medullary osmotic gradient? How does the countercurrent multiplier work? In what structure is the countercurrent multiplier found?

7. How does the countercurrent exchanger maintain the cortical to medullary osmotic gradient? In what structure is the countercurrent exchanger found?

8. How do the countercurrent multiplier and countercurrent exchanger contribute to the ability of the nephron to form concentrated urine? What other factors are involved in the ability of the nephron to form concentrated urine? What is the role that vasopressin plays in the concentrating ability of the nephron and how does vasopressin exert this effect?

9. What role does urea play in the ability of the nephron to form a concentrated urine?

10. How are the kidneys involved in the regulation of acid-base balance?

**Sample Handout to Facilitate Learning**

The following is an excerpt from a handout used to describe and explain the anatomy and physiology of the nephron. Students should be able to demonstrate a basic understanding of both the anatomy and physiology following a study of the handout and additional suggested readings. Handouts should be provided to the students about one week in advance of the class to allow sufficient time for reading of the material and for answering the Guided Learning Questions. This material can be posted to the institutional Learning Management System (LMS) so that students can download the material to their computers or print out a paper copy.

Handout excerpt:

## I. Review of Kidney Function

### A. <u>Introduction</u>

The kidneys excrete many of the end products of bodily metabolism. They also play a critical role in regulating the osmotic pressure, volume and ionic composition of the internal environment. The magnitude of the problem in the elaboration of urine is illustrated by the following considerations. Blood flow to both kidneys (in a 70 kg male) is approximately 1200 ml/min, which is approximately 20% of cardiac output. From this flow approximately 125 ml of glomerular ultrafiltrate are formed per minute, which has almost exactly the same composition as normal, protein free, interstitial fluid at pH 7.4. As the glomerular filtrate passes through the proximal tubules, about 60 to 70% of the filtrate is reabsorbed and almost all of the metabolically important substances (e.g., glucose, amino acids) are reabsorbed. By the time the fluid leaves the proximal tubules an average of 44 ml/min remains (isotonic solution). In its subsequent passage through the loop of Henle and distal nephron, the fluid is exposed to variable reabsorption and secretion of many different substances (e.g., $Na^+$, $Cl^-$, $HCO_3^-$, $K^+$, $H^+$, $H_2O$). These processes are normally regulated in accordance with the needs of the extracellular fluid. On average, urine is formed at a rate of 1 ml/min (can range from about 0.3 to 16 ml/min depending on the presence or absence of antidiuretic hormone (ADH/vasopressin)). Elaboration of urine is dependent on three discrete processes:

1. Glomerular ultrafiltration
2. Tubular reabsorption
3. Tubular secretion

These processes take place in each nephron (which is the functional unit) of the kidney.

### B. <u>Glomerular Ultrafiltration</u>

The glomerulus consists of Bowman's capsule and the tuft of capillaries formed from the afferent arteriole; this is the site at which formation of the ultrafiltrate occurs. The quantity of blood entering the kidneys every minute represents one-fifth of the resting cardiac output. Blood flows into the glomerulus via the afferent arteriole and exits via the efferent arteriole. As blood flows through the glomerular capillaries, about one-fifth of the plasma water passes through the capillaries and the glomerulus to enter the proximal portion of the renal tubule. The blood remaining in the vascular system enters the ...

## C. **Tubular Reabsorption**

1. More than 99% of the liquid filtered at the glomeruli is reabsorbed by the renal tubules. Much of the reabsorption occurs in the proximal tubule, i.e., approximately 60 to 70% of the filtered fluid is reabsorbed in the proximal tubule.
2. In general, most of the metabolically important substances, including glucose, amino acids, protein and Krebs cycle intermediates are reabsorbed in the proximal tubules.
3. $Na^+$ enters tubular cells at the brush border or luminal membrane by various mechanisms, but is actively transported out of the tubular cell at the basolateral membrane by a $Na^+$, $K^+$-exchange pump fueled by ATPase. In fact, the bulk of <u>all</u> transport in the kidney is due to an abundant supply of $Na^+$, $K^+$-ATPase in the basolateral membranes of renal epithelial cells. While $K^+$ is passively reabsorbed in the proximal tubule, it is both reabsorbed and secreted in the distal tubule. (The net flux of $K^+$ in the distal nephron is into the lumen of the tubule; that is, secretion). ...

## F. **Glomerulus and Proximal Tubule**

Glomerular filtrate initially contains about 300 mOsm/1 of solute (filtrate is isotonic, consisting primarily of $Na^+$, $Cl^-$ and $HCO_3^-$ ions). Reabsorption of ions and water from the filtrate occurs in the <u>proximal tubules</u> and may be characterized in the following manner:

1. Reabsorption is isosmotic.
2. Reabsorption of $Na^+$ is active at the basolateral membrane (via $Na^+$, $K^+$-ATPase). Three types of mechanisms are responsible at the

      luminal membrane for the movement of Na⁺ into the luminal cells: 1) diffusion with $Cl^-$; 2) cotransport or symport (CO in figure on following page) with uncharged molecules (such as glucose) or acidic anions (such as phosphate); 3) countertransport or antiport with hydrogen ion.

3. Reabsorption of $K^+$ is passive (about half of filtered $K^+$ is reabsorbed).

4. Reabsorption of $Cl^-$ is passive (against a small electrical gradient resulting from active egress of 3 $Na^+$ and uptake of 2 $K^+$, but down a concentration gradient).

5. Water is reabsorbed passively (due to osmotic force developed by active reabsorption of $Na^+$ at the basolateral membrane, and passive reabsorption of $Cl^-$). Under all conditions, <u>water diffuses readily in both directions across</u> the <u>proximal tubular epithelium</u>; therefore, the osmotic pressure of the tubular contents remains equal (isotonic) to that of plasma (approximately 300 mOsm/1).

As the filtrate flows along the proximal tubule, $Na^+$ is actively extruded into the interstitium while $K^+$ moves passively down its chemical gradient into the interstitium of the cortex; $Cl^-$ passively follows $Na^+$ and $K^+$, and water is reabsorbed by osmosis. The ions and water deposited in the interstitium are <u>rapidly</u> carried away by blood perfusing the cortical capillaries. Although the *volume is markedly reduced* at the beginning portion of the thin descending limb of the loop of Henle, the *fluid remains isotonic*. ...

(**END OF EXCERPT**).

## 4. How do you assess student learning?

Assessment of student learning is an ongoing process. Assessment takes place on a regular basis so that students understand what is expected of them. Assessments begin with the Individual Readiness Assurance Tests (IRATs). These quizzes are formative in that the students receive immediate feedback through discussions with their teammates and through the use of the IF-AT answer cards (as described above). The discussions of the RAT questions that take place between teammates results in students teaching and learning from each other. Further instructor led discussions lead to additional feedback through the explanation of fundamental concepts. Instructors do not move to the next question until all students understand the concept being illustrated in the RAT question.

Additional assessment occurs with the scoring of the application exercises. The use of an audience response system allows the responses from each team to be recorded and stored for scoring. These responses are not heavily weighted so that the responses to the application exercise questions are used for formation of a student's knowledge base. Furthermore, the discussion of the answers to the questions that takes place between teams allows additional opportunity for students to learn from each other.

Summative assessments of student learning takes place through the use of traditional multiple choice questions, short answer essays, oral questioning, the development of SOAP notes, and OSCE-type examinations. Essays, oral questions, SOAP notes, and OSCE-type exams are scored using rubrics. Rubrics should be made available to students in advance of the assessment so that they know what is expected of them and understand how their work is being assessed, scored and graded. Students have the opportunity to learn from these summative examinations through review of the examination with the instructor. This often helps clear up misunderstandings that students may still have regarding basic concepts of the material presented in the topic.

An example of an IRAT/TRAT that assesses whether or not students understand some of the fundamental concepts of nephron physiology follows:

1. The glomerular filtration rate (GFR) is influenced by

    I.   Pressure within the glomerular capillaries.
    II.  Hydrostatic within Bowman's capsule.
    III. Oncotic pressure within the glomerular capillaries.
    IV. A decrease in the cortical to medullary osmotic gradient.

    A. **I, II and III.**
    B. I and III.

    C. II and III.

    D. I and II.

    E. All influence glomerular filtration rate.

2. The majority of the metabolically important substances are

    A. Secreted into the lumen of the nephron in the proximal convoluted tubule.

    B. Reabsorbed from the lumen of the nephron in the distal convoluted tubule.

    C. **Reabsorbed from the lumen of the nephron in the proximal convoluted tubule.**

    D. Secreted into the lumen of the nephron in the thick ascending limb of the loop of Henle.

    E. Reabsorbed from the collecting tubules of the nephron.

3. The reabsorption of sodium from the lumen of the nephron to the interstitial fluid is driven by the

    A. Active reabsorption of $Cl^-$, which causes $Na^+$ to passively follow.

    B. Action of carbonic anhydrase, which actively pumps $HCO_3^-$ to the interstitial fluid causing $Na^+$ to passively follow.

    C. **$Na^+$-$K^+$-ATPase pump in the basolateral membrane of the epithelial cells, which establishes a concentration gradient for the movement of $Na^+$ from the lumen to the interstitial fluid.**

    D. Concentration gradient established by an increase in $Na^+$ reabsorption stimulated by aldosterone.

    E. Dilution of interstitial $Na^+$ by increased reabsorption of urea, which increases the concentration gradient for $Na^+$.

4. The cortical to medullary osmotic gradient in the kidney is *established* by the

    A. Countercurrent exchange mechanism present in the vasa recta.

    B.  Colloid oncotic pressure in the tuft of capillaries of the glomerulus.

    C.  Countercurrent exchange mechanism present in the loop of Henle.

    D.  Countercurrent multiplier mechanism present in the vasa recta.

    E.  **Countercurrent multiplier mechanism present in the loop of Henle.**

5.  Aldosterone increases the reabsorption of $Na^+$ from the

    A.  Descending limb of the loop of Henle.

    B.  **Late distal tubules and collecting ducts.**

    C.  Thick ascending limb of the loop of Henle.

    D.  Proximal convoluted tubules.

    E.  Tuft of capillaries of the glomerulus.

6.  The $Na^+$-$K^+$-$2Cl^-$ pump is located in the

    A.  **Luminal membrane of the epithelial cells of the thick ascending limb of the loop of Henle.**

    B.  Basolateral membrane of the epithelial cells of the late distal convoluted tubule.

    C.  Luminal membrane of the epithelial cells of the proximal convoluted tubule.

    D.  Cytoplasm of the epithelial cells of the collecting ducts.

    E.  Luminal membrane of the intercalated cells of the collecting ducts.

Following the TRAT, time may be spent going over concepts that appear to be confusing or not sufficiently grasped before moving on to an application exercise. Discussion also occurs after teams have completed the application exercise. This time is used for further explanation of basic concepts and for further elaboration of the fundamental concepts presented in the current classroom topic. During the discussion period, the instructor may use slides and other types of illustrations to elaborate on concepts and ask probing questions to engage the students in further learning of course content. This also gives the instructor the opportunity to model for the students the higher order thinking skills used in solving clinical cases.

Annotated Bibliography

1. Pathophysiology: Concepts of Altered Health States
   Edited by: Carol M. Porth, RN, MSN, PhD and Glenn Matfin BSc (Hons), MB, ChB, DCM, FFPM, FACE, FACP, FRCP, Eighth Edition, 2009, Wolters Kluwer Health | Lippincott Williams & Wilkins

   This textbook is written for nursing students but provides the conceptual foundation of pathophysiology for pharmacy students as well. The information is presented in at easily understandable level while maintaining an appropriate degree of detail. This information allows the pharmacy student an understanding of the pathophysiology without being overwhelmed by minute detail. Thus the pharmacy student can integrate physiology with the alterations from normal that occurs during diseases, that is, during altered health states. From understanding the alterations from normal physiological function that occurs during diseases students see the points of intervention for medical treatment of these conditions which provides a fundamental basis for understanding the functional mechanisms of action of pharmacological agents.

2. Pharmacology and Therapeutics: Principles to Practice
   Scott A. Waldman, MD, PhD, FCP and Andre Terzic, MD, PhD, 2009, Saunders Elsevier

   Although this text is rather detailed in the presentation of some topics, the authors provide an excellent integration of pathophysiology with pharmacology. This provides the instructor with a wealth of information that can be simplified for presentation to the students while offering a reference for those students who wish to delve into specific topics of their interest in greater detail.

3. Principles of Pharmacology: The Pathophysiologic Basis of Drug Therapy,
   David E. Golan, MD, PhD, Armen H. Tashjian, Jr, MD, Ehrin J. Armstrong, MD, MSc, April W. Armstrong, MD, Third Edition, 2011, Wolters Kluwer Health | Lippincott Williams & Wilkins

   This textbook provides another version of the integration of pathophysiology with pharmacology for the treatment of these conditions. The textbook offers the instructor conceptual information for presentation to pharmacy students while giving pharmacy students a source that integrates pathophysiology with pharmacology.

# CHAPTER 3

# Pharmacology
## *Rajat Sethi, Ph D*

In this chapter, the backward design model is used to create a TBL unit on cardiovascular pharmacology with emphasis on hypertension. The ultimate aim of therapy is to reduce elevated blood pressure, which would ultimately lead to end-organ damage. The goal is achieved through the use of various drug classes, and treatment often involves a combination of agents. In order to fully comprehend the pharmacological effects of commonly used anti-hypertensive agents and identify effective strategies for the clinical management of hypertension, the student must *know* the anatomy of the vasculature and etiology of hypertension, *understand* the principles of blood pressure regulation, *predict* the responses mediated by the sympathetic and renin angiotensin system on blood pressure, *identify* the determinants of systemic blood pressure, and *recognize* the significance of compensatory responses to antihypertensive treatments. The integration of anatomy and physiology forms the foundation for understanding the pathophysiology of hypertension, and pathophysiological concepts are integrated with the pharmacology of antihypertensive agents in the design of therapeutic regimens for patients with high blood pressure.

What follows is a description of the development of a course topic on the pharmacology of hypertension using the backward design model.

1. **What do you want your students to be able to do when they have finished the course or course topic?**

When students finish this course they should be able to accomplish the following course learning outcomes:

1. Explain the etiology and pathophysiology of various cardiovascular disease states.
2. Discuss the physiological significance of cardiac, vascular, renal, and neuroendocrine function in relation to heart failure, cardiac arrhythmias, ischemic heart disease, hypertension, and hyperlipidemia.
3. Describe the pharmacological effects, mechanisms of action, and the adverse effects of the medications used to treat cardiovascular disorders.
4. Discuss the basis for combination therapies in the treatment of cardiovascular disease states.

The learning outcomes for a course topic should align with the course learning outcomes. The learning outcomes on hypertension pharmacology are as follows:

1. Describe and discuss the anatomy and physiology of the cardiovascular system.
2. Explain the etiology and pathophysiology of cardiac and vascular function.
3. Describe the mechanisms of action and the adverse effects of the medications used to treat vascular disorders that effect blood pressure.

**Application Exercises (IBAT)**

Application exercises for this unit are design to build skills at a gradual pace. The discussion after each application exercise can also be used to increase the knowledge base of students by expounding and elaborating on fundamental concepts. Thus discussion points are an important component of the IBAT.

### Application 1: Understanding the determinants (factors) of Systemic Blood Pressure (SBP)

What would happen to SBP (↑, ↓ or 'no effect') with increases in?

Cardiac Output       _____

Heart Rate       _____

Stroke Volume       _____

Contractility       _____

Preload       _____

Venous Tone       _____

Intravascular Volume       _____

Systemic Vascular Resistance       _____

Afterload       _____

### Discussion Points

As these factors are interrelated, students should be able to:

- Identify determinants which are important parameters for cardiac, vascular, renal and neuroendocrine function?
- Which of the determinants indirectly alter blood pressure through other determinants?

## *Application 2: Understanding the homeostatic mechanisms in Systemic Blood Pressure (SBP)*

[*PNS-parasympathetic nervous system; *SNS-sympathetic nervous system; RAS- renin angiotensis system; ADH- anti diuretic hormone; NO- nitric oxide; ATII- angiotensin II]

<u>What would happen to SBP (↑, ↓ or 'no effect') with increased?</u>

PNS activity      _____

SNS activity      _____

Catecholamine Secretion      _____

Aldosterone      _____

ADH Secretion      _____

Natriuretic Peptides      _____

NO      _____

Prostacyclin      _____

Endothelin      _____

Adenosine      _____

RAS/AT II      _____

Oxygen      _____

Alpha1 adrenergic receptor stimulation      _____

## Discussion Points

As the determinants of SBP are altered by a number of homeostatic factors, students should be able to:

- Discuss the effects of these factors on various determinants
- How do these factors alter blood pressure?

### Application 3: Based on the understanding of concepts in application 1 & 2, please identify the determinants and the factors of SBP which are altered by the following antihypertensive drugs

Beta Blockers       _____

Calcium Channel Blockers       _____

Alpha1Blockers       _____

Sodium Nitroprusside       _____

ACE Inhibitors       _____

ATII Antagonists       _____

Diuretics       _____

Endothelin Antagonists       _____

Central alpha2 agonists       _____

## Discussion Points

Antihypertensive agents modulate SBP by altering the factors that control BP. Students should be able to:

- Discuss the basic absorption, distribution, metabolism and excretion of these drugs?
- Identify the adverse effects associated with these drugs?
- Elaborate on the basis for combining vasodilators with beta blockers and diuretics to preserve the effectiveness of vasodilator therapy.

*Application 4: Based on the understanding of concepts in applications 1, 2 and 3, please identify the drug of choice and the rationale for its selection in the following cases:*

<u>Case 1:</u> John is an elderly white male with 5 year history of hypertension. He is currently on a combination of enalapril and hydrochlorthiazide for his hypertension. His BP is still elevated at 165/94 mm Hg. Other vitals include a HR 85 beats/min, and RR 14 breaths/min. He has a serum creatinine (Cr) of 1.52 mg/dL and and serum potassium ($K^+$) of 5.0 mEq/L. Metoprolol therapy is being considered.

**Questions:**

1. *What is the rationale for starting metoprolol in this patient?*
2. *When should metoprolol be initiated?*

<u>Case 2:</u> Susana is a 60 year old female patient who visits the clinic for newly diagnosed hypertension. She suffers from angina and has asthma. Her vital signs are: BP 160/99 mm Hg, HR 55 beats/min, and RR 16 breaths/min. She is on albuterol for her asthma, and nitroglycerine sublingual tablets for angina. She is started on a calcium channel blocker to control her BP.

**Questions:**

1. *What is the rationale for using a calcium channel blocker as the initial treatment for this patient? When should metoprolol be initiated?*
2. *What antihypertensive agents are relatively contraindicated in this patient?*

**Case 3:** Nicole is a 64 year old woman with newly diagnosed hypertension. She also suffers from osteoporosis. Her current medications include calcium carbonate, estrogen, and medroxyprogesterone acetate. Her vital signs are: BP 162/70 mm Hg, HR 65 beats/min, RR 18 breaths/min. Her renal function is within normal limits and she has no signs of fever.

**Questions:**

1. *Is thiazide diuretic appropriate as initial treatment for this patient? Provide rational.*
2. *Why or why not?*

2. **What will your students need to know in order to be able to do those things?**

   1. The common determinants which effect SBP.
   2. The homeostatic mechanisms in SBP.
   3. The commonly used drugs for decreasing hypertension and how they affect the determinants and the homeostatic mechanisms in SBP.
   4. The mechanisms of action, therapeutic uses, adverse effects, contraindications, and pharmacokinetics of commonly used antihypertensive drugs.

3. **How do you facilitate student learning?**

Students learn by accomplishing specific learning objectives and answering probing questions as they review and study pre-class assignments. A handout is provided to focus the learning on various aspects that must be learned in order to accomplish the learning objectives. What follows is a list of questions students should be able to answer after reading the handout.

*Guided Learning Questions*

   1. What are the common determinants of systemic blood pressure (SBP)?

2. What are the common homeostatic mechanisms affecting the determinants of SBP?

3. What are the various classes of antihypertensive drugs?

4. What are the pharmacological effects and mechanisms of actions of commonly used antihypertensive drugs?

5. What are the similarities and differences in mechanisms of action, therapeutic uses, pharmacokinetics, and adverse effects of terazosin and other alpha adrenergic blockers?

6. What are the similarities and differences in mechanisms of action, therapeutic uses, pharmacokinetics, and adverse effects of thiazide, loop and potassium sparing diuretics?

7. What are the similarities and differences in mechanisms of action, therapeutic uses, pharmacokinetics, and adverse effects of various beta-adrenoceptor blocking agents?

8. What are the similarities and differences in mechanisms of action, therapeutic uses, pharmacokinetics, and adverse effects of angiotensin converting enzyme inhibitors and angiotensin receptor II blockers?

9. What are the various classes of calcium channel blockers, and the similarities and differences in the mechanisms of action, therapeutic uses, pharmacokinetics, and adverse effects between these classes?

10. What drugs are used for hypertensive emergencies, and what is their mechanism of action?

## _Guided Learning Handout_

A succinct handout describing the major aspects of the topic is provided to students to help them address the questions above. Students are also directed to use specific chapters of textbooks to help them address these questions.

## 4. How do you assess student learning?

Here are some typical Individual readiness assessment tests/team readiness assessment tests (IRAT/TRAT) multiple choice questions that assesses whether or not students understand some of the fundamental concepts from the reading. The IRAT gives individual students formative feedback on how well they grasped the fundamental concepts. The TRAT allows students to discuss the answers they gave on their IRAT and must reach a consensus on what is the right answer. During these discussions, students teach each other basic concepts and delve into a greater depth of understanding.

1. An elderly patient had controlled BP of 140/86 mm Hg while on furosemide, atenolol, and loratadine for 6 months. He ran out of his medication for one week. He is now experiencing high blood pressure (173/99 mm Hg). His past medical history (PMH) includes hypertension, asthma, and diabetes. What is the most likely reason for his increased BP?

   A. **Rebound Hypertension**
   B. Antihypertensive medication not adequate
   C. Loratadine
   D. Hyperglycemia
   E. Ashthma

2. An 89 year old patient presents to the clinic with untreated hypertension and a PMH of coronary artery disease, myocardial infarction, chronic obstructive pulmonary disease, and renal impairment. There is a strong indication for initiating which of the following beta-blocker in this patient?

   A. Atenolol
   B. Nadolol
   C. **Metoprolol**
   D. Propranolol
   E. Labetolol

3. An elderly women on calcium channel blockers for her blood pressure reveals that she has been having problems with constipation since starting therapy. In addition she complains

of her "gum" swelling. Which of the following calcium channel blocker is the most likely cause of her side effects?

A. Diltiazem
B. **Verapamil**
C. Amlodipine
D. Nifedipine
E. Losartan

4. Which of the following antihypertensive drugs may cause a precipitous fall in blood pressure on initial administration?

A. Atenolol
B. **Prazosin**
C. Metoprolol
D. Verapamil
E. Captopril

5. Mike is a 56 year old male patient with hypertension and renal insufficiency [Creatinine clearance (CrCl) 20L/min]. He presents to the clinic with elevated BP of 160/93 mm Hg. Which of the following diuretic is probably not effective in this patient?

A. Furosemide
B. Bumetanide
C. Torsemide
D. **Hydrochlorthiazide**
E. Losartsan

6. Which of the following antihypertensive agents can precipitate a hypertensive crisis following abrupt cessation of therapy after prolonged administration?

A. **Clonidine**
B. Diltiazem
C. Losartan
D. Hydrochlorthiazide

  E.  Metorpolol

7.  An elderly male patient presents to the clinic complaining of
    headache and dizziness. His sitting and standing BP are BP 95/62
    mm Hg and HR 110 beats/min. He was started on the ACE
    inhibitor benazepril 10 days ago. His PMH includes hypertension
    and osteoarthritis. Labs include a serum sodium <128 mEq/L,
    serum potassium (K$^+$) 4.6 mEq/L, and creatinine (Cr) 1.1 mg/
    dL. What is/are the risk factors for ACE inhibitor-induced
    hypotension?

    A.  Hyponatremia (Serum Sodium < 130 mEq/L)
    B.  Concurrent diuretic use
    C.  Concurrent NSAID use
    D.  A, B & C
    E.  **A & B only**

8.  Which of the following is true for beta blockers used to treat
    hypertension?

    A.  Increase heart rate
    B.  Decrease renin release
    C.  Decrease contractility
    D.  Increase sympathetic activity
    E.  **B & C only**

9.  Which of the following mechanisms listed are not related to the
    actions of vasodilators?

    A.  Release of nitric oxide from endothelium
    B.  Reduction of calcium influx
    C.  Activation of dopamine receptors
    D.  **Increased sympathetic nervous system outflow**
    E.  C and D only

10. Thiazide diuretics decrease blood pressure by:

A. **Decreasing peripheral resistance**
B. Increasing cardiac output
C. Increasing blood volume
D. Increasing sodium water retention
E. A and D only

**Annotated Bibliography:**

Basic and Clinical Pharmacology;

Edited by: Bertram G. Katzung, MD, PhD, Susan B. Masters, PhD, Anthony J. Trevor, PhD, 12th Edition, 2012, McGraw Hill.

This book is designed to provide a comprehensive, easy to read pharmacology textbook for health professional students. The information provided is an integration of the physiology of the human system, pathophysiology of the disease state, and pharmacology of drugs, helping students learn pharmacology in a conceptual framework that fosters mechanism-based learning rather than crude memorization.

# CHAPTER 4

# Pathophysiology and Therapeutics
## *David Hawkins, Pharm D*

The topic of type 2 diabetes mellitus will be used to illustrate how a TBL unit can be designed for a course in pathophysiology and therapeutics.

1. **What do you want your students to be able to do when they have finished the course or course topic?**

   1. Design and defend a therapeutic plan for a patient with diabetes mellitus based on relevant pathophysiologic and pharmacologic mechanisms and co-morbid conditions;
   2. Identify and manage common adverse effects associated with sulfonylureas, biguanides, glitazones, glucosidase inhibitors, dipeptidyl peptidase-IV inhibitors, incretins, amylin receptor agonists, and insulin; and
   3. Evaluate patients with diabetes mellitus to assess disease progression, pathophysiologic complications, and response to therapy.

The following is an example of a case study that requires students to demonstrate that they understand the pathophysiology of type 2 diabetes, how to treat this condition, and how to evaluate a patient's response to treatment.

**Patient Case**

Louise Jackson is a 49-year-old woman who presents to her primary care physician with complaints of increasing fatigue, hunger, thirst, and urination. She states her last appointment with her primary care physician was less than 6 months ago. At that visit, blood work was done that revealed normal hemoglobin and hematocrit, normal serum electrolytes, normal kidney function, and a blood glucose of 160 mg/dL about two hours after lunch. A lipid blood panel revealed a total cholestrerol of 260 mg/dL, HDL cholesterol of 60 mg/dL, and a triglyceride of 300mg/dL. The patient has a history of hypertension for the past three years.

Both the patient's mother and older sister have diabetes. Her father died suddenly of a heart attack at the age of 59. She has been married for 20 years and has three children. She works full-time as a bank teller. Her husband is a used car salesman. She denies alcohol or tobacco use. She rarely exercises and admits to trying several different diets to lose weight but with not much success.

Mrs. Jackson reports that she takes 25 mg of hydrochlorothiazide daily. She does not complain of any eye symptoms, chest pain, tingling or numbness in her legs, or foot problems.

Her vital signs revealed a blood pressure of 160/90, a pulse rate of 80 beats per minute, and a respiratory rate of 12 breaths per minute. She weighs 160 pounds and is 5'6" tall. Her physical exam was completely normal except for several exudates noted on funduscopic exam in both eyes. Her fasting blood glucose concentration is 180 mg/dL and her hemoglobin A-1C level is at 8%.

## Assignment

1. Write out your assessment of this patient's presenting signs, symptoms, abnormal lab values, and concomitant conditions and explain how you reached your assessment.
2. Write out a plan for managing this patient's presenting problems and defend your plan by providing both the pathophysiologic and pharmacologic *rationale.*

**2. What will your students need to know in order to be able to do those things?**

Fundamental concepts are the basic units of knowledge upon which in-depth learning is constructed. To master the topic of diabetes, students will need to grasp and understand the following three basic fundamental concepts:

- pathophysiologic mechanisms and complications of diabetes,
- pharmacologic mechanisms and adverse effects of all medications used to lower serum glucose concentration, and
- physical assessment methods needed to evaluate the disease state and clinical response to treatment.

Once the concepts have been identified, a set of specific learning objectives can be written that if accomplish will enable a student to grasp and understand fundamental concepts. There are usually 1 to 3 learning objectives for each fundamental concept. Learning objectives for diabetes might include the following:

1. Describe the mechanisms involved in the pathogenesis and pathophysiology of type 1 and type 2 diabetes mellitus;
2. Indicate how diabetes causes retinopathy, neuropathy, and nephropathy;
3. Explain why diabetes leads to the development or worsening of coronary artery disease, peripheral vascular disease, and hypertension;
4. Describe the mechanism of action of insulin and all oral agents used to treat diabetes and what effect the pharmacologic action has on pathophysiologic mechanisms;
5. Identify the side effects associated with each class of oral antidiabetic medications and the mechanism responsible for the side effects;
6. Indicate the starting doses of antidiabetic medications, how to titrate the dose, and what combination of agents can be used when monotherapy is insufficient;

7. Formulate the rationale and method of initiating lifestyle modifications;
8. Recognize the onset and manage the acute complications of diabetes (diabetic ketoacidosis and hyperosmolar hyperglycemic state).
9. Recognize the occurrence and manage the chronic complications of diabetes (retinopathy, neuropathies, nephropathy, hypertension, and coronary artery disease); and
10. List the clinical and laboratory parameters for evaluating a patient with diabetes and response to treatment.

## 3. How do you facilitate student learning?

One of the best ways to facilitate student learning is to provide students with a handout that identifies what specifically they should learn and a set of probing questions that guides their learning. We refer to this as a guided learning handout.

Here is an example of a guided learning handout for the topic of diabetes.

### I. Pathogenesis

    A. Type 1 DM
    B. Type 2 DM

*What is the cause of type 1 and type 2 DM?*

### II. Diagnosis

    A. Impaired fasting glucose
    B. Impaired glucose tolerance
    C. Diabetes mellitus

*How are the above three conditions diagnosed?*

## III. Clinical Presentation

    A.  Signs

    B.  Symptoms

*What are the signs and symptoms of DM?*

    C.  Acute complications

    D.  Chronic complications

*What acute and chronic complications occur in type 2 DM?*

## IV. Approach to the Patient

    A.  History

    B.  Physical

*What factors need to be emphasized in taking a history from a patient with a confirmed or presumptive diagnosis of DM?*

*What should the physical exam specifically focus on in a patient with DM?*

    C.  Treatment Goals

*What are the A1C, FBS, postprandial BG, BP, and lipid goals for patients with DM?*

    D.  Nutrition

*What are the nutritional recommendations for adult patients with DM regarding fat, carbohydrate, protein, fiber, and sweeteners?*

## V. Pharmacotherapy Management

    A.  Insulin therapy

*Complete the following table:*

| Type of Insulin | Onset (minutes/ hours) | Peak (hours) | Duration (hours) |
|---|---|---|---|
| **Rapid-acting** | | | |
| Aspart (*NovoLog*) | | 0.5-1.5 | 3-5 |
| Lispro (*Humalog*) | 5-15 minutes | | 3-5 |
| Glulisine (*Apidra*) | 5-15 minutes | 0.5-1.5 | |
| **Short-Acting** | | | |
| Regular (U-100) | 30-60 minutes | | 4-8 |
| **Intermediate-acting** | | | |
| NPH | | 4-10 | 10-18 |
| Concentrated Regular (U-500)** | 30-60 minutes | Varies | |
| **Long-acting** | | | |
| Detemir (*Levemir*) | 1-3 hours | minimal | |
| Glargine (*Lantus*) | 2-4 hours | | 20-24 |

**What is the initial insulin dosage regimen for a patient with type 2 DM?**

    B.  GLP-1 agonists

This injectable class of incretin mimetics enhances glucose dependent insulin secretion while suppressing postprandial glucagon excursions; does not suppress glucagon secretion during hypoglycemia; reduces food intake and slows gastric emptying; no weight gain; nausea/vomiting common side effects; minimal hypoglycemia unless combined with insulin or sulfonylurea; rare but serious warnings include pancreatitis, medullary thyroid cancer (noted in mouse model), and renal impairment.

Exenatide (*Byetta*): inject 5-10 mcg SC bid, within the 60 minute period before meals. Avoid in renal disease [ClCr < 30 mL/min].

Exenatide ER (*Bydureon*): inject 2 mg SC weekly, without regard to meals. Avoid in renal disease [ClCr < 30 mL/min].

Liraglutide (*Victoza*): Inject 0.6-1.8 mg daily, without regard to meals. No dosage adjustment for renal impairment.

C. Amylin Mimetic

Pramlintide (*Symlin*): Enhances glucose dependent insulin secretion while suppressing postprandial glucagon excursions; does not suppress glucagon secretion during hypoglycemia; reduces food intake and slows gastric emptying; peak 20 minutes, duration 3-4 hrs, metabolized by kidneys; nausea/vomiting common side effects; dose 60-120 mcg prior to major meals in type 2 and 15-60 mcg in type 1. Insulin doses generally should be reduced with the initiation of pramlintide to avoid hypoglycemia.

D. Oral Glucose Lowering Agents: ***Complete the following table.***

| Oral Agent | Trade Name | Dosage Range (mg) | Duration of Action (Hrs) |
|---|---|---|---|
| ***Insulin Secretagogue***s | | | |
| Chlorpropamide | | 100-500 | >48 |
| Tolazamide | | | 12-24 |
| Tolbutamide | | | 6-12 |
| Glimepiride | | 1-8 | 24 |
| Glipizide | | | 12-18 |
| Glipizide ER | | 5-10 | 24 |
| Glyburide | | | 12-24 |
| Glyburide micronized | | 0.75-12 | 12-24 |
| Repaglinide | | | 2-6 |
| Nateglinide | | | 2-4 |
| ***Biguanides*** | | | |

| Metformin | | | |
|---|---|---|---|
| Metformin ER | | | 24 |
| *Thiazolidinediones* | | | |
| Pioglitazone | | | 24 |
| Rosiglitazone | | 2-8 | 24 |
| *Glucosidase Inhibitors* | | | |
| Acarbose | | 25-100 | 1-3 |
| Miglitol | | | 1-3 |
| *DPP IV Inhibitors* | | | |
| Sitagliptin | | 25-100 | 24 |
| Saxagliptin | Onglyza | | |
| Linagliptin | Tradjenta | | |
| | Nesina | 6.25-25 | |

*What is the pharmacologic mechanism of action of the five different classes of oral glucose lowering agents?*

*What are the major side effects of the five different classes of oral glucose lowering agents?*

**VI. Management of Diabetic Complications**

    A. **Cardiovascular Disease**

        1. Hypertension

- Target SBP < 140 and DBP < 80. Consider lower targets as comorbid conditions dictate (e.g. SHF, CAD, MI, CKD, ischemic stroke, AAA, or Framingham risk >20%). Be aware these targets may change with new evidence and updated guidelines. See ADA, AHA, and JNC for updates.

- Focus on lifestyle medication (e.g. weight loss, nutrition, moderate exercise).
- Multiple drug therapy is often required to reach goal. ACE-I or ARBs, CCBs, and thiazide diuretics are all effective choices. ACE-I or ARBs preferred if comorbid renal disease or proteinuria present.
- Small glucose changes may be observed with the initiation of diuretics or beta-blockers. Generally these changes are clinically insignificant.
- Non-selective beta-blockers may mask hypoglycemia in patients taking insulin or secretagogues. Caution with medications like propranolol and carvedilol.

2. Dyslipidemia

- Focus on lifestyle modification and statin therapy to lower LDL initially.
- LDL < 100mg/dL, or < 70mg/dL in patients with overt CVD.
- Consider combination therapy if goals are not met, although mortality benefits not as clearly documented as with statin therapy.
- TG < 150 mg/dL, or non-HDL < (LDL target + 30 mg/dL).
- For patients with TG > 1000 mg/dL, there is concern for developing acute pancreatitis. Consider fibrates, fish oil (4000 mg in divided doses), or insulin to rapidly lower TGs between visits. Niacin may also be considered but titration is slow, flushing may not be tolerated, and niacin may elevate BG levels at high doses.
- Statin therapy is also recommended for all patients over the age of 40 with DM regardless of LDL if tolerated.

## B. Nephropathy

A1C reduction and BP control also help prevent progression. In the treatment of non-pregnant patients with micro- (ACR > 30) or macroalbuminuria (ACR > 300), either ACE-I or ARB (monitor serum creatinine and potassium). Untreated, leads to dialysis.

## C. Retinopathy

Annual screening. A1C reduction prevents progression. Vision may be preserved with laser photocoagulation. Untreated, leads to blindness.

## D. Neuropathy

1. Distal symmetric polyneuropathy

   - Optimal glycemic control
   - Tricyclic antidepressants (amitriptyline, nortriptyline, imipramine)
   - Anticonvulsants (gabapentin, carbamazepine, pregabalin)
   - 5-HT and NE reuptake inhibitor (SNRI such as duloxetine)
   - Substance P inhibitor (capsaicin cream)

2. Autonomic neuropathy

   - Gastroparesis – metoclopramide or erythromycin
   - ED – phosphodiesterase 5 inhibitors (sildenafil, vardenafil, tadalafil)
   - Cardiac neuropathy may elevate resting HR and cause postural hypotension.

## 4. How do you assess student learning?

What follows is an example of a readiness assurance test for the topic of diabetes. The correct answers are in bold font.

1. Which pathophysiologic abnormalities usually coincide with new onset type 2 diabetes?

I.   Reduced insulin secretion
II.  Insulin resistance
III. Excessive hepatic glucose production

    A. I only
    B. II only
    C. I and II only
    D. **II and III only**
    E. I, II, and III

2. Based on the underlying pathophysiology of type 2 diabetes, the most appropriate pharmacologic treatment to initiate is:

    A. Insulin
    B. A sulfonylurea agent like glyburide
    C. **Metformin**
    D. A thiazolidinedione such as rosiglitazone
    E. Sitagliptin

3. What would you recommend for a patient with type 2 diabetes and heart failure on combination of metformin and glyburide with the following blood glucose ranges: before breakfast 110-120 mg/dL, before lunch 120-130 mg/dL, mid-afternoon 190-210 mg/dL, and bedtime 185-195 mg/dL?

I.   Pioglitazone
II.  Sitagliptin
III. Glargine injection before meals

    A. I only
    B. **II only**
    C. I or II only
    D. II or III only
    E. I, II, or III

4. Sulfonylurea agents lower blood glucose by:

   I. Increasing insulin sensitivity
   II. Increasing insulin secretion
   III. Activating $K^+$/ATP channel on pancreatic B cells

   A. I only
   B. II only
   C. I and II only
   D. **II and III only**
   E. I, II, and III

5. Which regimens have demonstrated benefit for patients with pre-diabetes?

   I. Diet and exercise
   II. Metformin
   III. TZDs

   A. I only
   B. II only
   C. I or II only
   D. II or III only
   E. **I, II, or III**

**Annotated Bibliography**

*Pharmacotherapy: A Pathophysiologic Approach, Eight Edition,* Joseph T. DiPiro, Robert L. Talbert, Gary C. Yee, Gary Matzke, Barbara Wells, and L. Michael Posey, editors, The McGraw-Hill Companies, Inc., 2011.

This textbook book summarizes the epidemiology, classification, diagnosis, pathophysiology, and treatment of disease states and provides a detailed description of therapeutic information including pharmacology, pharmacokinetics, efficacy, adverse effects, drug interactions, and dosing and administration information. Each chapter of the book also discusses key concepts of the disease state, goals of therapy, and treatment strategies.

*Harrison's Principles of Internal Medicine, Eighteenth Edition*, Dan L. Longo, Anthony S. Fauci, Dennis L. Kasper, Stephen L. Hauser,, J. Larry Jameson, and Joseph Loscalzo, editors, The McGraw-Hill Companies, Inc., 2012.

This textbook covers the classification, epidemiology, diagnosis, pathogenesis, complications, approach to the patient, and treatment of diseases.

# CHAPTER 5

# Clinical Toxicology
## *Grant Lackey, Pharm D*

In this chapter, the backward design model is used to create a TBL unit for a clinical toxicology course. The unit chosen to illustrate the model is the toxicology of digitalis.

Cardioactive steroids such as digoxin remain in wide use throughout the world, although their benefits have become more and more restricted. Many poisonings have occurred with exposures to plants such as Digitalis purpurea and Nerium oleander containing cardioactive steroids, which are used by herbalists for varied disorders. Recent abuse of dried toad secretions that contain cardioactive steroids has also led to high morbidity and mortality. Rapid recognition of cardioactive steroid toxicity and appropriate use of digoxin-specific antibody fragments can prove lifesaving. For a student to fully understand digitalis toxicity, he or she must have a working knowledge of the pharmacology, pharmacokinetics, and pharmacodynamics of digitalis. This knowledge base is needed to determine the seriousness of a digitalis exposure and to design an appropriate therapeutic plan for treating acute or chronic toxic exposure to digitalis. This knowledge base is also necessary for interpreting blood levels of digitalis for deciding on the use and calculating the dose of digoxin-specific antibody fragments.

What follows is a list of learning outcomes, a case study or application exercise, specific learning objectives, guided learning materials, and assessments of student learning for the topic

4.  **What do you want your students to be able to do when they have finished the course or course topic?**

When students finish this course, they should be able to accomplish the following course learning outcomes:

1.  Review, describe, and discuss the basic pathophysiology, pharmacology, and toxic syndromes associated with potentially life threatening and commonly seen poisoning exposures.
2.  Explain the methods used for the decontamination of patients with common poisonings.
3.  Explain and evaluate the available antidotes used in common poisoning exposures.
4.  Describe and evaluate a treatment plan and end points of therapy for commonly seen poisonings.

The learning outcomes for a course topic should align with the course learning outcomes. The learning outcomes for the digitalis toxicity course topic are as follows:

1.  Review, describe, and discuss the basic pathophysiology, pharmacology, pharmacokinetics, and pharmacodynamics of digitalis.
2.  Explain the major toxic reactions from a chronic and an acute toxic digitalis exposure.
3.  Describe and evaluate a therapeutic treatment plan for digitalis toxicity including decontamination, the proper use of digoxin immune fragments, and the endpoints of therapy.

**Application Exercise:**

The application exercise below can be provided to students before class to assist in their topic preparation.

R.W. is a depressed mechanic being treated for atrial fibrillation. He recently received a prescription of 60 digoxin 0.25 mg tablets and was instructed to take one daily. He told his roommate that he ingested all 60 of his digoxin tablets about 2 hours ago and was feeling very lethargic and nauseated. His roommate called 911. The paramedics arrived, checked his circulation, secured his airway, and administered 50 grams of activated charcoal. The patient was transported to the emergency department for evaluation and treatment. In the emergency department he presented confused and lethargic. Atropine was administered without any changes.

**Past medical history:** Depression and atrial fibrillation **Current Medications:** Digoxin

The patient was experiencing mild pain and was combative and confused. He had a temperature of 96.9F.

**Physical examination:** Blood pressure 110/70, respiratory rate 18 breathes/minute an irregularly irregular heart rate of 50 beats/minute and bibasilar rales. An EKG showed bradycardia with 3rd degree heart block, unresponsive to atropine. His oxygen saturation rate was 96%

**Laboratory results:** Digoxin level 3.0 ng/ml. Serum electrolytes included a potassium of 5.2, sodium of 142, chloride of 114, and a bicarbonate of 24. Arterial blood gases indicated a PaCO2 of 38, Pa02 of 75, pH of 7.45. Renal function indicated a serum creatinine of 1.2 and a blood urea nitrogen of 8.

1. What are the most immediate and chronic concerns in this patient?
2. Was the use of activated charcoal appropriate?
3. At this point, what would you do for this patient?
4. What laboratory studies would you order for this patent?
5. What is the pathophysiological basis of toxicity in this patient?
6. What is your treatment plan?

## IBAT/TBAT

The questions listed below could be presented to individual students first (IBAT) and then to each team (TBAT). For the TBAT, the teams will simultaneously report their answer to each question. The instructor will call on a team to defend its answer and then ask other teams with different answers to present their argument for choosing an alternative answer. This will engage the class in debate. The instructor will then discuss with the class their reasoning and help the class think through the arguments to reach the right answer to the question.

1. Upon arrival to the emergency department, the physician ordered all the appropriate laboratories, an EKG, and a serum digoxin level. What would you expect the digoxin level to be?

   a. In a toxic range
   b. Sub-therapeutic
   c. Within the therapeutic range
   **d. Unable to determine**

2. If R.W. was confused and his roommate determined that he had ingested the digoxin tablets at least 6-8 hours prior to arrival of the paramedics, what would you expect the digoxin level to be?

   **a. In a toxic range**
   b. Sub-therapeutic
   c. Within the therapeutic range
   d. Unable to determine

3. The assessment of the severity of digoxin toxicity should include all of the following except:

   a. Renal function
   b. Electrolytes
   **c. Liver function**
   d. Electrocardiogram
   e. Serum Digoxin Level

4. The toxic syndrome associated with an acute exposure to digoxin can include all the following except:

   **a. CNS excitation.**

b. Visual disturbances
c. Nausea and vomiting
d. Life threatening arrhythmias

5. Assessment of R.W.'s digoxin ingestion should include the following:

   i.   Accidental ingestion - unintentional or deliberate overdose
   ii.  Altered digoxin metabolism due to diminished renal clearance
   iii. Digoxin interactions with other drugs.

   F. I only.
   G. I and II.
   H. I and III.
   I. II and III.
   **J. I, II and III.**

6. The mechanism of action of cardiac glycosides includes:

   i.   Direct vasodilation in the arterial and venous system in vascular smooth muscle
   ii.  Direct inhibition of membrane-bound sodium- and potassium-activated adenosine triphosphates (Na+/K+ -ATPase), which leads to an increase in the intracellular concentration of calcium
   iii. Associated increase in a slow inward calcium current during the action potential

   F. I only.
   G. I and II.
   H. I and III.
   **I. II and III.**
   J. I, II and III.

7. After administration of digoxin immune fragments, digoxin drug levels should be evaluated based upon

a. **Free digoxin levels.**
b. Bound digoxin levels.
c. Total free and bound digoxin levels.

8. In evaluating the changes in electrolytes that can occur in patients with elevated digoxin levels one should keep in mind:

   I. Hyperkalemia frequently occurs in patients with acute digoxin poisoning.
   II. Hypokalemia can occur in patients who are on chronic diuretic therapy with acute and chronic digoxin poisoning.
   III. Hypercalcemia can occur in patients who are on chronic calcium channel blocker therapy with chronic digitalis poisoning.

   A. I only.
   **B. I and II.**
   C. I and III.
   D. II and III.
   E. I, II and III.

9. Digoxin immune Fab is considered the first-line treatment for significant dysrhythmias from digitalis toxicity. Other indications for its use include:

   I. Ingestion of massive quantities of digitalis >10mg
   II. Serum digoxin levels greater than 10 ng/mL in adults at steady state
   III. Hyperkalemia (serum potassium level greater than 5 mEq/L)
   IV. Altered mental status attributed to digoxin toxicity

   a. I only.
   b. I and II.
   c. I and IV.
   d. II and III.
   **e. I, II, III, and IV.**

10. Digoxin levels in acute exposures:

    I.   Peak in 6-8 hours from time of ingestion.

    II.  Are in the distribution phase for the first hour after the exposure.

    III. Are in distribution phase and peak in 12 hours.

    A.  I only.
    **B.  I and II.**
    C.  I and III.
    D.  II and III.
    E.  I, II and III.

## 2. What will your students need to know in order to be able to do those things?

Students will need to understand the fundamental concepts of the pharmacology, pharmacokinetics, and the pharmacotherapeutics of digoxin and other cardioactive steroids in order to accomplish the learning outcomes listed under Step 1. The following learning objectives will help students grasp and understand the concepts.

1. Describe the basic pharmacology and pharmacokinetics of cardioactive steroids.
2. List the similarities and differences of the symptoms between an acute digoxin exposure and a chronic digoxin exposure.
3. List the methods used for gut decontamination in acute cardioactive steroid exposures.
4. List and describe the indications for the use of Digoxin Immune Fab Fragments as an antidote for elevated digoxin levels.
5. List the endpoints of therapy.

## 3. How do you facilitate student learning?

A guided learning handout can be provided to focus the learning on those aspects that must be learned in order to grasp and understand the fundamental concepts. It is important to learn about the source, amount, time of ingestion, presence of any co-ingestant, and patient's comorbidities. Acute digitalis toxicity can result from unintentional, suicidal, or homicidal overdose of the digoxin or accidental ingestion of plants that contain cardiac glycosides. Chronic toxicity in patients on digoxin therapy may result from deteriorating renal function, dehydration, electrolyte disturbances, or drug interactions. Alterations in cardiac rate and rhythm from digitalis toxicity may simulate almost every known type of dysrhythmia.

**Handout example:**

### Cardioactive Steroids: Digoxin Overdose

The following questions can be used to guide student learning.

1. What are the symptoms of an acute exposure to cardioactive steroids?
2. What are the syptoms of a chronic exposure to cardioactive steroids?
3. What are the methods of gut decontamination that can be used for acute cardioactive steroid exposures?
4. How do you determine the appropriate time to obtain a digoxin level?
5. How do you interpret a digoxin level?
6. What are the indications for the use of digoxin-specific antibody fragments?
7. What is the role of dialysis in cardioactive steroid exposures?
8. What are the endpoints of antidote therapy?

**Signs and symptoms**

Digitalis toxicity can produce extra-cardiac and cardiac manifestations.

CNS symptoms of digitalis toxicity may include drowsiness, lethargy, fatigue, neuralgia, headache, dizziness, confusion, hallucinations, seizures, paresthesia, neuropathic pain, visual changes such as yellow-green halos, and photophobia. GI symptoms in either acute or chronic toxicity can include nausea, vomiting, diarrhea, anorexia, abdominal pain, and weight loss. Cardiac symptoms may include bradycardia, hypotension, palpitations, syncope, and shortness of breath.

## Diagnosis

- Studies in patients with possible digitalis toxicity include serum digoxin level, electrolytes, renal function studies, ECG, and serum digoxin levels (therapeutic levels are 0.6-1.3.)
- Levels determined less than 6-8 hours after an acute ingestion do not necessarily predict toxicity.
- The best way to guide therapy is to follow the digoxin level and correlate it with serum potassium concentrations and the patient's clinical and ECG findings.
- In acute toxicity, hyperkalemia is common. Chronic toxicity is often accompanied by hypokalemia and hypomagnesaemia.
- Digoxin toxicity may cause almost any dysrhythmia. Classically, dysrhythmias associated with increased automaticity and decreased AV conduction can occur. Nonparoxysmal atrial tachycardia with heart block and bidirectional ventricular tachycardia are particularly characteristic of severe digitalis toxicity.

## Emergency Management

Supportive care of digitalis toxicity focuses on:

- Airway, circulation, and breathing.
- Oxygenation and support of ventilator function as needed.
- Correction of electrolyte imbalances as needed.

    o   For hyperkalemia, use insulin plus glucose, and sodium bicarbonate if the patient is acidotic (usually used in an acute intoxication)

- ○ Correct hypokalemia (usually used in a chronic intoxication, digoxin does not directly cause hypokalemia, it is commonly a result of the poly-pharmacy use of diuretics)
- ○ Concomitant hypomagnesemia may result in refractory hypokalemia

- GI decontamination

  - ○ Activated charcoal is indicated for acute overdose or accidental ingestion.
  - ○ Binding resins (eg, cholestyramine) or multiple dose activated charcoal may be indicated as digoxin may be enterohepatically recirculated.

- Treatment with digoxin Fab fragments is indicated for a K+ level greater than 5 mEq/L.
- Hemodialysis may be necessary for uncontrolled hyperkalemia.

**Digoxin immune Fab**

Digoxin immune Fab is considered the first-line treatment for significant dysrhythmias from digitalis toxicity. Other indications for its use include:

- ingestion of massive quantities of digoxin (10 mg in adults)
- serum digoxin levels greater than 10 ng/mL in adults at steady state (ie, 6-8 hours after acute ingestion or at baseline in chronic toxicity)
- hyperkalemia (serum potassium levels greater than 5 mEq/L)
- altered mental status
- any progressive signs and symptoms of cardioactive steroid toxicity

**Management of dysrhythmias**

In hemodynamically stable patients, bradyarrhythmias and supraventricular arrhythmias are usually treated with supportive care.

- supraventricular tachyarrhythmia with rapid ventricular rates - consider short-acting beta blockers (eg, esmolol) Note: can precipitate advanced or complete AV block in patients with sinoatrial or AV node depression.
- ventricular tachycardia if digoxin Fab fragment therapy is ineffective or unavailable - consider phenytoin and lidocaine. Phenytoin can suppress digitalis-induced tachydysrhythmias
- severe sinus bradycardia - consider atropine.
- magnesium sulfate may terminate dysrhythmias (contraindicated in the setting of bradycardia or AV block and should be used cautiously in patients with renal failure)
- cardioversion for severe dysrhythmias

## End of Handout Excerpt

## 4. How do you assess student learning?

Assessments begin with the Individual Readiness Assurance Test (IRAT). During the Team Readiness Assurance Test (TRAT), the discussions of the RAT questions that take place between teammates results in students teaching and learning from each other. The teams receive immediate feedback from the IFAT cards they use to mark their answers. Further instructor led discussions lead to additional feedback through the explanation of fundamental concepts.

Additional assessment occurs with the scoring of the application exercises. The use of an audience response system allows the responses from each team to be recorded and stored for scoring. These responses are not heavily weighted so that the responses to the application exercise questions are used for formation of a student's knowledge base. Furthermore, the discussion of the answers to the questions that takes place between teams allows additional opportunity for students to learn from each other.

Summative assessments of student learning takes place through the use of traditional multiple choice questions, short answer essays, oral questioning, the development of SOAP notes, and OSCE-type examinations. Essays, oral questions, SOAP notes, and OSCE-type exams are scored using rubrics. Rubrics should be made available to students in advance of the assessment so that they know what is expected of them and understand how their work is being assessed, scored and graded. Students have the opportunity to learn from these summative examinations through review of the examination with the instructor. This often helps clear up misunderstandings that students may still have regarding basic concepts of the material presented in the topic.

Following the TBAT, time may be spent going over concepts that appear to be confusing or not sufficiently grasped before moving on to an application exercise. Discussion also occurs after teams have completed the application exercise. This time is used for further explanation of basic concepts and for further elaboration of the fundamental concepts presented in the current classroom topic. During the discussion period, the instructor may use slides and other types of illustrations to elaborate on concepts and ask probing questions to engage the students in further learning of course content. This also gives the instructor the opportunity to model for the students the higher order thinking skills used in solving clinical cases.

**Annotated Bibliography**

1. <u>Poisoning and Drug Overdose, 6e</u>, edited by: Kent Olsen, MD, 6<sup>th</sup> Edition, 2011, Chapter 61 Digoxin and Cardio glycosides, Lange, McGraw Hill <u>Poisoning and Drug Overdose</u> provides practical advice for the diagnosis and management of poisoning and drug overdose and information about common industrial chemicals. It is written as a concise manual for emergency departments but provides the conceptual foundation of pharmacotherapy and basic pathophysiology for professional students in toxicology. The information is presented at an easily understandable level while maintaining an appropriate degree of detail. The manual is divided into four sections and is designed to allow the reader to move quickly from one section to another while obtaining needed information. The information presented allows the

health professions student to gain an understanding of the pharmacotherapy and basic pathophysiology of various poisoning and drug overdose conditions without being overwhelmed by minute detail.

2. Goldfrank's Toxicologic Emergencies, Ninth Edition by Lewis Nelson, Neal Lewin, Mary Ann Howland and Robert Hoffman, 2010, McGraw-Hill Although this textbook is rather detailed in the presentation of some topics in toxicology, the authors provide an excellent integration of toxicology, pharmacology, and pathophysiology of the poisoned patient. This provides the instructor with the opportunity to focus on various toxic substances that can then be simplified for presentation to the students while offering a reference for those students who desire greater detail.

# CHAPTER 6

# Biostatistics
## *Robert Clegg, Ph D*

The course in biostatistics is designed to prepare the student to critically assess the results of statistical analysis reported in the medical literature. The benefits and pitfalls of using statistical software will also be covered. A section covering pharmacoepidemiology will focus on methods for discovering, reporting, and appraising adverse drug events. This course will provide students with an understanding of probability concepts, distributions of random variables, nonparametric methods, and other statistical methods used in biomedical, pharmaceutical, and health care research. Emphasis is on thinking about research issues in a statistically sound and practical fashion. Moreover, students will learn how to formulate and ask the right questions, collect data properly, summarize and interpret information, understand the limitations of statistical inferences, and obtain an understanding of the concepts of statistical reasoning as applied to the study of clinical problems. This includes learning basic terminology and its meaning, the calculations of various statistical measures and indices, quantification of health relationships, and the interpretation of inferential statistical techniques.

1. **What do you want your students to be able to do when they have finished the course or course topic?**

The student learning outcomes for this course topic are as follows:

1. Describe the role of data analysis in the research process;
2. Describe the differences between descriptive and inferential statistical analysis and differentiate between the four levels of measurement;

3.  Analyze a visual display of data and interpret measures of central tendency and variability;
4.  Describe the standard normal distribution and the two types of errors that are present in hypothesis testing, and interpret both clinical and statistical significance;
5.  Differentiate between parametric and nonparametric statistics and interpret the results of various types of statistical tests in health care research.

For the purpose of the Guide, we have chosen the unit on the fundamental concepts related to calculating the mean, standard deviation, quartiles and interquartile range (IQR), formulating a boxplot, and hypothesis testing to illustrate how such a topic can be built on a Team-Based Learning (TBL) frame using the backward design model presented in Chapter 1.

The student learning outcomes for this unit are as follows:

1.  Define, discuss, and calculate the most commonly encountered measures of central tendency - the mean, median, and mode;
2.  Understand the concept of variation among a group of scores including understanding the standard deviation and how to calculate it;
3.  Draw and understand figures/graphs that display several different measures of central tendency representing different treatment conditions or groups; and
4.  Use the range to compare the spread of two sets of data.
5.  Use hypothesis testing to test a mean or proportion.

What follows is an application exercise that is first carried out by each individual student (IBAT) and then completed by each team (TBAT).

## IBAT/TBAT

*Cryptosporidium parvum* outbreaks are commonly associated with contaminated drinking supplies and swimming pools. The incubation period for the disease is normally about 1–12 days with an average of about

7 days. You have been assigned to find the sample standard deviation for incubation periods for 10 cases of infectious cryptosporidiosis discovered at a large metropolitan waterpark. The incubation periods for the 10 identified cases are as follows:

| 6.5 | 6.6 | 6.7 | 6.8 | 7.1 | 7.3 | 7.4 | 7.7 | 7.7 | 7.7 |

1. Calculate the mean ($\bar{x}$) and sample standard deviation ($s$) of the 10 incubation periods.

| Observations $x_i$ | Deviations $(x_i - \bar{x})$ | Squared Deviations $(x_i - \bar{x})^2$ |
|---|---|---|
| 6.5 | 6.5 – 7.15 = -0.65 | 0.4225 |
| 6.6 | 6.6 – 7.15 = -0.55 | 0.3025 |
| 6.7 | 6.7 – 7.15 = -0.45 | 0.2025 |
| 6.8 | 6.8 – 7.15 = -0.35 | 0.1225 |
| 7.1 | 7.1 – 7.15 = -0.05 | 0.0025 |
| 7.3 | 7.3 – 7.15 = 0.15 | 0.0225 |
| 7.4 | 7.4 – 7.15 = 0.25 | 0.625 |
| 7.7 | 7.7 – 7.15 = 0.55 | 0.3025 |
| 7.7 | 7.7 – 7.15 = 0.55 | 0.3025 |
| 7.7 | 7.7 – 7.15 = 0.55 | 0.3025 |
| $\bar{x}$ = **7.15** | | $\Sigma$ = 2.6075 |

$\Sigma(x_i - \bar{x})^2 = 2.6075$

$s^2 = \Sigma(x_i - \bar{x})^2 / (n - 1) = 2.6075 / 9 = 0.289$

$s = \sqrt{s^2} = \mathbf{0.538}$

2. Calculate the quartiles and the interquartile range (IQR) from the 10 identified cases of infectious cryptosporidiosis, then formulate a boxplot based on these calculations below:

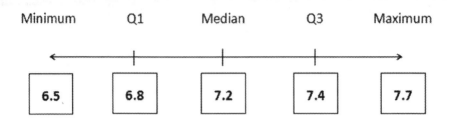

IQR (Maximum – Minimum) = **1.2**

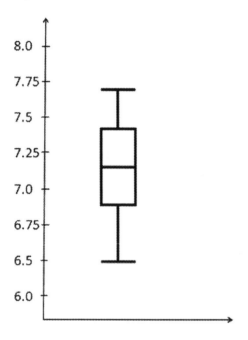

## 2. What will your students need to know in order to be able to do those things?

The pre-class assignment is for students to read and study Chapter 8 – *Hypothesis Testing* in the recommended text ***Basic Statistics and Pharmaceutical Statistical Applications* (2nd ed.)** by James E. De Muth. After completing the reading assignment, the students should be able to:

1. Define the basic principles of hypothesis testing;

2. Describe the null hypothesis and alternative hypothesis and their role in hypothesis testing;
3. Determine the sample size for a given hypothesis test;
4. Distinguish Type I and Type II errors in statistical inference;
5. Interpret the confidence level, significance level, and power of a test;
6. Compute and interpret *P*-values.

## 3. How do you facilitate student learning?

Coupled with the TBL methodology, this course uses the Teaching and Learning Model, which contains three key elements: a) Active Learning, b) Collaboration, and c) Emphasis on Application and Relevance. First and foremost, faculty members are expected to serve not only as teachers, but also as facilitators in the learning process. This process is managed by engaging students in a variety of activities that enhance understanding which, in turn, develops academic and professional competence. Second, by encouraging and facilitating collaboration, it adds a robust dimension to the learning process by allowing students to teach and learn from one another. Lastly, research has shown that the best learning occurs when there is a connection between new knowledge and the student's experience, hence adding relevance to the educational experience. The goal for the third element of the Model is for students to apply what they have learned in class in their respective place of employment the following day.

A guided learning handout is provided to focus student learning with regard to the fundamental concepts of hypothesis testing as it relates to biostatistics. In order to allow sufficient time for reading of the material and to answer the guided learning questions, guided learning handouts are provided to the students one week in advance of the class. The following questions can be used to guide student learning in Chapter 8 of the required text:

1. How is statistical significance different from clinical significance? Provide examples of each.
2. What is statistical power? Provide examples of where it is used.

3. With the help of examples from healthcare, explain the difference between one-sided and two-sided statistical tests.

4. Use a pharmaceutical example to explain why a null hypothesis is either rejected or not rejected, but is never accepted.

5. If power is calculated to be 85%, with Type I error rate of 5%, what are then percentages associated with the four possible outcomes associated with hypothesis testing? What if the power was only 72%?

6. In a randomized, controlled trial of preemptive analgesia in men who underwent radical prostatectomy surgery, functioning was statistically ($\alpha = 0.05$) and clinically significantly improved in men who received the experimental treatment compared to men who received usual care. What can be said about the assessment of statistical significance in this case?

7. Suppose the normal level of hemoglobin (Hb) in children is 13.2 g/dL. A study on a random sample of 10 children with chronic diarrhea revealed that the mean is 12.6 g/dL and the standard deviation is 1.77 g/dL. The objective is to determine whether children with chronic diarrhea, on average, have less Hb level or not. State the null hypothesis and alternative hypothesis for this study.

## 4. How do you assess student learning?

The IRAT/TRAT on hypothesis testing will focus on the general principles of statistical testing, which includes defining hypothesis, null hypothesis ($H_0$), and alternative hypothesis ($H_1$), power, $P$-value, Type I error ($\alpha$-error), Type II error ($\beta$-error), and level of significance (alpha level, $\alpha$).

IRAT/ TRAT

Hypothesis Testing

1. Type I error occurs when

   a. the null hypothesis is accepted.
   b. the null hypothesis is accepted when false.
   c. the null hypothesis is rejected.

    **d. the null hypothesis is rejected when true.**

    e. None of the above.

2. Pfizer asserts that its new beta-blocker medication is definitely more effective than the existing drug in the market for controlling hypertension. In order to verify this claim, your null hypothesis would be that the new drug has

    a. more efficacy than the existing drug.

    **b. the same efficacy as the existing drug.**

    c. less efficacy than the existing drug.

    d. no effect.

    **e. There is not enough data to develop a null hypothesis based on the information provided.**

3. The *P*-value is the probability of

    a. not rejecting a null hypothesis when true.

    b. rejecting a null hypothesis when false.

    **c. rejecting a null hypothesis when true.**

    d. not rejecting a null hypothesis when false.

    e. None of the above.

4. A clinical trial was conducted on 25 patients with a new antihyperlipidemic drug and another 25 patients on placebo. The difference found is as much as 30% in the efficacy but it is not statistically significant. This can happen due to all of the following EXCEPT:

    **a. high Type I error.**

    b. small sample size.

    c. lack of power.

    d. high Type II error.

    e. None of the above.

5. Statistical significance does NOT imply that

    **a. the difference has arisen by chance.**

    b.  *P*-value is less than the level of significance.

    c.  the probability of a true hypothesis being rejected is small.

    d.  the difference is likely to persist from sample to sample.

    e.  None of the above.

6.  A prospective, randomized, double-blind study ($n = 2,400$) finds that when two oral drugs for treating type 2 diabetes mellitus are compared, the final mean percent hemoglobin A1C value is 7.41 for patients in Group 1 and 7.37 for patients in Group 2. This difference between the groups is stated as having a calculated *P*-value less than 0.05. Assuming similar baseline characteristics and appropriate final statistical analysis, which one of the following statements best characterizes these findings?

    a.  The difference between the drugs is clinically, but not significantly, significant.

    b.  The difference between the drugs is both statistically and clinically significant.

    **c.  The difference between the drugs is statistically, but not clinically, significant.**

    d.  The difference between the drugs is neither statistically nor significantly significant.

    e.  None of the above.

7.  The probability of Type II error is called

    a.  Alpha.

    **b.  Beta.**

    c.  Power

    d.  *P*-value.

    e.  Level of significance.

8.  A randomized clinical trial comparing efficacy of two regimens of an inhaled corticosteroid showed that the difference is significant with $P = 0.02$. But in reality, the two drugs do not differ in their efficacy. This is an example of

a. **Type I error (α-error).**
b. Type II error (β-error).
c. $1 - \alpha$.
d. $1 - \beta$.
e. None of the above.

9. All of the following are true EXCEPT:

   a. When *P*-value is more than the level of significance, it is said to be statistically not significant. Level of significance is predetermined, whereas *P*-value is obtained on the basis of data.
   b. Type I error in a trial set-up means that a new regimen, although not effective, is adopted and prescribed. This is a serious error.
   c. **Power is the complement of probability of Type II error (e.g., power = 1 – β).**
   d. Type II error is also called a beta error.
   e. All of the above is true.

10. A clinical trial compares Drug A and Drug B for treating patients with Cystic Fibrosis (CF) because clinicians believe they differ in their efficacy in the treatment of wheezing and shortness of breath. Drug A has been used for many years and has a large evidence base showing efficacy and safety. Drug B was recently introduced to treat chronic obstructive pulmonary disease (COPD), but it has not been well studied in patients with CF. Patients will be randomized to one of these two drugs. Which one of the following represents the correct statement of the null hypothesis for this trial?

    a. **The efficacy of Drug A equals the efficacy of Drug B.**
    b. The efficacy of Drug A does not equal the efficacy of Drug B.
    c. The efficacy of Drug A is greater than the efficacy of Drug B.
    d. The efficacy of drug X is less than the efficacy of drug Y.
    e. There is not enough data to develop a null hypothesis based on the information provided.

**Annotated Bibliography**

*Basic Statistics and Pharmaceutical Statistical Applications* (2nd ed.), James E. De Muth, 2006.

The first edition of *Basic Statistics and Pharmaceutical Statistical Applications* successfully provided a practical, easy-to-read, basic statistics book. This second edition not only updates the previous edition, but expands coverage in the area of biostatistics and how it relates to real-world professional practice. Taking you on a roller coaster ride through the world of statistics, Dr. De Muth clearly details the methodology necessary to summarize data and make informed decisions about observed outcomes.

*Biostatistics for Medical, Nursing and Pharmacy Students*, Abhaya Indrayan & L. Satyanarayana, 2006.

Designed especially for undergraduate students in medicine, pharmacy and nursing, this compact text, oriented completely to the medical aspects, skillfully analyzes the fundamentals of biostatistics. The book begins with discussions on biostatistics in health and diseases, types of data, and methods of data collection. Then it goes on to give a detailed description of fertility and demography indicators, indicators of social and mental health, sampling, standard error and confidence interval, as well as the principles of statistical tests. The study concludes with a discussion on parametric and non-parametric tests, chi-square tests, regression and correlation, and sample size in medical studies.

*Clinical Pharmacist's Guide to Biostatistics and Literature Evaluation*, Robert DiCenzo (ed.), 2011.

Whether you are interpreting the medical literature to optimize patient care, improve health outcomes, or generate hypothesis for research, an understanding of biostatistics is essential for success. This book was developed to bolster the pharmacist's knowledge and confidence for using biostatistical tools for interpreting the literature. With material drawn from ACCP's renowned Pharmacotherapy Self-Assessment Program (PSAP) and the live pharmacotherapy preparatory course Updates in Therapeutics, editor Robert DiCenzo, Pharm.D., FCCP, BCPS, has designed this review to support pharmacists' preparation for the Pharmacotherapy and Ambulatory Care Board of Pharmacy Specialties (BPS) examinations.

*Handbook of Basic Statistical Concepts for Scientists and Pharmacists*, Shubha Rani, 2012.

Explains the fundamentals of frequently used statistical methods including distributions, estimation, testing of hypothesis, correlation and regression in a very simple and understandable language. An attempt is made to emphasize the importance of identifying the problem correctly and applying appropriate statistical methods. Various examples are given to demonstrate the application of different statistical techniques depending upon the situation and pertaining objectives. It will help in developing both an understanding and appreciation of the discipline. Though the book is written with the aim of explaining basic statistical concepts to scientists and students of pharmacy, it will be useful for readers from any field or background.

# CHAPTER 7

# Clinical Epidemiology
## *David Hawkins, Pharm D*

The course in clinical epidemiology is designed to teach students how to apply epidemiologic methods to analyze, evaluate, and make clinical decisions that improve patient care. Clinical epidemiology deals specifically with clinical questions pertaining to abnormality, diagnosis, risk, prevention, prognosis, treatment, and cause.

**1. What do you want your students to be able to do when they have finished the course or course topic?**

The student learning outcomes for the course are as follows:

1.  Formulate the various types of questions clinicians need to answer in taking care of patients.
2.  Recognize the various criteria used in clinical medicine for distinguishing normality form abnormality.
3.  Define the various properties of a diagnostic test and calculate the sensitivity, specificity, positive and negative predictive values, and likelihood ratios for a given diagnostic test.
4.  Calculate estimates of risk from prospective observations and retrospective studies.
5.  Outline different strategies for determining relative risk, attributable risk, relative odds, and etiologic fraction and indicate how these are used in making clinical decisions.
6.  Design a study to determine both the clinical efficacy and clinical effectiveness of a therapeutic intervention.
7.  Evaluate the evidence of causation based on validating criteria.

For the purpose of the Guide, we have chosen the unit on diagnosis to illustrate how such a topic can be built on a TBL frame using the backward design model presented in Chapter 1.

The student learning outcomes for the diagnosis unit are:

1.  Describe how the accuracy of a diagnostic test is established.
2.  Discuss why sensitivity is more important than specificity for screening tests.
3.  Discuss why specificity is more important than sensitivity for confirming a diagnosis.
4.  Explain how receiver operator characteristic (ROC) curves can be used to choose a cut-point between normal and abnormal.
5.  Explain how predictive values and likelihood ratios are used to guide treatment decisions.

What follows is an application exercise that is first carried out by each individual student and then completed by each team.


**IBAT/TBAT**


A study was done to determine the ability of clinicians to diagnose venous thromboembolism (DVT) in 100 patients who presented to the emergency room complaining of swelling and pain in a lower extremity. The doctors' clinical impressions were compared to results of compression ultrasonography. Thirty patients had positive ultrasound results and of these 15 were diagnosed by the doctors' clinical impressions. Seventy patients had negative ultrasounds. Doctors diagnoses 35 of these as having DVT.

1.  What is the sensitivity of the doctors' clinical impression of DVT in this study?
2.  What is the specificity?
3.  If the doctor thought that the patient had a DVT, for what percent of patients was she correct?

4. If the doctor thought the patient did not DVT based on the clinical exam, for what percent of the patients was he correct?
5. How common was DVT in patients coming to the ER complaining of swelling and pain in the calf?
6. How confident would you be to start treatment on a patient with a doctor's diagnosis of DVT based on the clinical exam only?

## IBAT/TBAT Answers

|  |  | Ultrasonography Results | |
|---|---|---|---|
|  |  | Positive | Negative |
| Diagnosis | Positive | 15 | 35 |
|  | Negative | 15 | 35 |

1. **Sensitivity** = 15/30 or 50%
2. **Specificity** = 35/70 or 50%
3. **Positive Predictive Value** = 15/50 or 30%
4. **Negative Predictive Value** = 35/50 or 70%
5. **Prevalence** = 30/100 or 30%

## 2. What will your students need to know in order to be able to do those things?

The pre-class assignment is for students to read and study Chapter 3 *Diagnosis* from the required text *Clinical Epidemiology: the Essentials* by Robert Fletcher and Susan Fletcher. After completing the reading assignment, the students should be able to:

1. Define the fixed properties of a diagnostic test (sensitivity and specificity)
2. Answer the following questions regarding the sensitivity of a diagnostic test:

    a. Why is a high level of sensitivity desirable for a test that is used to screen for the presence of a disease?

    b. Why is a sensitive test more useful than a specific test when the differential list includes multiple possibilities?

3. Indicate why a high level of specificity is desirable for a test that is used to confirm the presence of a disease?
4. Explain how ROC curves can be used to establish cutoff points for a diagnostic test and to visualize the relationship between sensitivity and specificity for a diagnostic test.
5. Correctly interpret diagnostic tests for distinguishing normality from abnormality and for making appropriate treatment decisions and:

    a. define positive and negative predictive value;
    b. explain the relationship between accuracy and positive and negative predictive values;
    c. explain how positive and negative predictive values are calculated;
    d. explain how likelihood ratios are used to describe the performance of a diagnostic test; and
    e. explain how likelihood ratios are calculated.

6. Use multiple tests to guide treatment decisions and:

    a. explain why it is often necessary for a clinician to order multiple tests to rule in or rule out the presence of disease;
    b. describe what parallel testing is and its effect on sensitivity/specificity and negative/positive predictive value; and
    c. describe what serial testing is and its effect on sensitivity/specificity and negative/positive predictive value.

## 3. How do you facilitate student learning?

This class will focus on how diagnostic tests are established and how test data should be interpreted. These are important topics as common questions that health care providers ask are: 'How accurate are tests that are used to diagnose patients?' or 'If a test is positive, how likely is it that my patient has the disease in question?' We will also discuss how to appropriately relay test data and its meaning to patients and other health care professionals. You should read and study Chapter 3 in ***Clinical Epidemiology: The Essentials, 4th Edition by Robert H. Fletcher and Suzanne W. Fletcher, Lippincott Williams & Wilkins, 2005.*** The handout below is provided to help guide your study of this topic.

### *Guided Learning Handout on Diagnostic Tests*

You should be able to answer the following questions after reading and studying the required text:

1. What is the sensitivity of a diagnostic test and how do you calculate it?
2. What is the specificity of a diagnostic test and how do you calculate it?
3. What three reasons dictate the use of a diagnostic test with a high sensitivity index?
4. What two reasons dictate the use of a diagnostic test with a high specificity index?
5. Once the results of a diagnostic test are known, the question arises as to how predictive are the results. What type of diagnostic test has a better positive predictive value and what type of diagnostic test has a better negative predictive value?
6. How do you calculate positive and negative predictive values?
7. While sensitivity and specificity are fixed properties of a diagnostic test, predictive values are affected by the prevalence of disease in question. When do the positive and negative predictive values approach 0?
8. Given the following data, calculate the positive and negative predictive values of the diagnostic test for a disease that is 50% prevalent and for a disease that is 10% prevalent.

| Test Result | Disease Present | Disease Absent | Predictive Value |
|---|---|---|---|
| Positive | 400 | 50 | |
| Negative | 100 | 450 | |

| Test Result | Disease Present | Disease Absent | Predictive Value |
|---|---|---|---|
| Positive | 80 | 90 | |
| Negative | 20 | 810 | |

9. Likelihood ratios (LR) indicate the odds that a given level of a diagnostic test would be expressed in a patient with as opposed to one without the target disorder. How do you calculate the LR for a positive test? How do you calculate the LR for a negative test?

10. How do you calculate the pretest odds of having a target disorder based on its probability in a given subject? How do you then calculate the posttest odds of having the disorder in question? How do you convert posttest odds back to probability?

11. A 45 year old woman with a history of chest pain has a pretest probability of coronary artery disease (CAD) of 1%. A careful history reveals that the patient's chest pain is substernal, radiates down the left arm, is brought on by exertion, and is relieved by rest. The positive LR of such a history in a woman has been calculated to be 120. Based on this LR what is now her probability of having CAD?

An exercise tolerance test (ETT) is ordered for the patient to help confirm the diagnosis. Her ETT showed a 2.2 mm ST segment depression. The LR of this ETT result in a woman has been calculated to be 11. What is now her probability for having CAD?

## 4. How do you assess student learning?

The IRAT/TRAT on diagnosis focuses on the fundamental properties of a diagnostic test and the interpretation of test results.

### IRAT/ TRAT Diagnosis

1. The property of a diagnostic test that is defined as the proportion of people with the disease who have a positive test for the disease is called:

   A. Sensitivity
   B. Specificity

   C. Positive predictive value
   D. True positive rate minus false positive rate
   E. Accuracy

2. The property of a diagnostic test that is defined as the proportion of people without the disease who have a negative test is called:

   A. Sensitivity
   B. Specificity
   C. Negative predictive value
   D. True negative rate minus false negative rate
   E. Accuracy

3. A diagnostic test with a high degree of sensitivity:

   I.   Is useful when there is an important penalty for missing a disease
   II.  Is useful when the differential list includes multiple possibilities
   III. Is most helpful in ruling out disease when the test result is negative

      A. I only
      B. II only
      C. I and II only
      D. II and III only
      **E. I, II, and III**

4. A diagnostic test with a high degree of specificity:

   I.   Is useful to rule-in a diagnosis when the test result is positive
   II.  Is useful when the differential list includes multiple possibilities
   III. Is most helpful in ruling out disease when the test result is negative

      **A. I only**
      B. II only
      C. I and II only
      D. II and III only
      E. I, II, and III

5. A receiver operator characteristic (ROC) curve is useful for:

    I.   Choosing between a diagnostic test that is highly sensitive from one that is highly specific
    II.  Choosing cut-off points between normal and abnormal
    III. Choosing a diagnostic test that is both sensitive and specific

    A. I only
    **B.** II only
    C. I and II only
    D. II and III only
    E. I, II, and III

6. The predictive value of a diagnostic test is determined by:

    I.   Subtracting the true positive rate from the false positive rate
    II.  The sensitivity and specificity of the test
    III. The prevalence of the disease in the population being tested

    A. I only
    B. II only
    C. I and II only
    **D.** II and III only
    E. I, II, and III

7. Which of the following parallelisms is true?

    I.   The more sensitive a test the better will be its negative predictive value
    II.  The more specific a test the better will be its positive predictive value
    III. The more sensitive a test the better will be its positive predictive value

    **A.** I only
    B. II only
    C. I and II only

    D.  II and III only
    E.  I, II, and III

8.  The positive likelihood ratio for a particular value of a diagnostic test is defined as:

    I.   Sensitivity divided by 1-specificity
    II.  Sensitivity minus specificity
    III. 1 minus sensitivity divided by specificity

    A.  I only
    B.  II only
    C.  I and II only
    D.  II and III only
    E.  I, II, and III

9.  The benefit of using likelihood ratios in making a diagnosis is:

    I.   Determining the odds that a given range of test results would be expressed in a patient with (as opposed to one without) the disease in question
    II.  Overcoming the limitation of sensitivity and specificity
    III. Describing the overall odds of a disease when a series of diagnostic test is used

    A.  I only
    B.  II only
    C.  I and II only
    D.  II and III only
    E.  I, II, and III

10. A 65 y/o woman is in the hospital complaining about calf pain. Her probability of having a DVT is 50%. Physical exam reveals that she has a positive Homan's sign which is associated with a LR of 1.5. Given that LR, what is now her probability of having a DVT? The patient undergoes venography that indicates a positive test result. The LR of a

positive venogram in such a patient is 40. What is now her probability of having a DVT?

A. 25%
B. 35%
C. 50%
D. 75%
**E.** 98%

## Annotated Bibliography

*Clinical Epidemiology: The Essentials,* Robert H. Fletcher and Susan W. Fletcher, Williams & Wilkins, 2013

This book is a comprehensive review of the principles of evidence-based medicine needed to make and evaluate clinical decisions. The book is organized around the major clinical issues and questions that should be considered in the provision of patient care.

# CHAPTER 8

## Creating a Team-Based Learning Pedagogical Culture
### David Hawkins, Pharm D

In this chapter we discuss what it takes to create and maintain a TBL pedagogical culture and some of the lessons we learned while developing an entire pharmacy didactic curriculum on a TBL frame.

### The Paradigm Shift

The first step in transforming the lecture hall into an active learning classroom is instigating a paradigm shift in how faculty view teaching and learning. In the 1960's, the National Training Laboratories in Bethel, Maine reported on the estimated average retention rates associated with different teaching methods. The associations are illustrated in the following diagram, which has become known as the learning pyramid:

**Leads to Passive Learning**

**Leads to Active Learning**

**Learning Pyramid**

| Lecture | 5% |
| Reading Text | 10% |
| Audio-Visual | 20% |
| Demonstration | 30% |
| Discussion group | 50% |
| Learning by doing | 75% |
| Teaching others | 90% |

Average retention of material presented in different ways

Some have argued that the percentages shown in the diagram above were not obtained from a proper experiment but stem from a simplistic approach to describing a rather complex process. Nevertheless, it seems logical that the best way to retain what you learn is to teach others, to apply what you learn, and to discuss the things you are learning with a group of fellow learners. This is what TBL is all about. Faculty need to spend more time designing instruction that encourages students to teach each other fundamental course concepts, requires students to apply what they are learning to analyze problems, synthesize solutions, and evaluate outcomes (higher order thinking), and involves students in group discussions. These are all effective ways to engage students in active learning.

Listening to a lecture, reading chapters in textbooks, watching videos, or observing demonstrations are not all bad. However, such forms of passive learning encourage rote memorization, discourage critical thinking, and impede the construction of knowledge.

Some of the erroneous assumptions about lecturing include the notion that knowledge can be directly transmitted to students, that it is more important to cover content than to teach fundamental concepts, and that students are impressed with a faculty member's knowledge, expertise, and ability to entertain the class. The only thing transmitted during a lecture is information. Students work hard to capture every word the instructor speaks thinking that exam questions will flow directly from the lecture. As far as being compelled to "cover the content" goes, the only way to learn is to think through content. It is more important to guide students in learning fundamental concepts than covering lots of content. When students are required to apply those concepts to a case study, clinical problem, or probing question they become engaged in critical and higher order thinking which leads to active learning and knowledge retention.

Therefore, a paradigm shift must occur in the pedagogical approach faculty take toward teaching and learning, as summarized below.

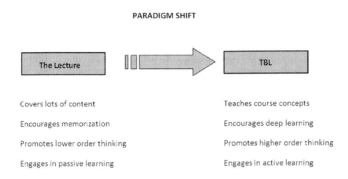

PARADIGM SHIFT

| The Lecture | TBL |
| --- | --- |
| Covers lots of content | Teaches course concepts |
| Encourages memorization | Encourages deep learning |
| Promotes lower order thinking | Promotes higher order thinking |
| Engages in passive learning | Engages in active learning |

## Faculty Development

It is probably safe to say that most faculty in pharmacy were never taught how to teach before they entered their academic careers. What they typically do when they first start out teaching is imitate their former instructors, most, if not all, of whom taught by lecturing. Therefore, a faculty development program directed toward training faculty how to teach is imperative. The program required to train faculty on how to design and deliver a team-based learning course is much more rigorous and labor intensive than a program for developing good lecturers. We would recommend the following faculty development workshops:

1. **Basic Training in TBL** – This workshop focuses on teaching the basic concepts of team-based learning. This includes proper formation of teams, defining learning outcomes, developing application exercises, writing readiness assurance questions, and preparing pre-class assignments. There are many experts in the field of TBL who can facilitate this workshop. You can visit the Team-Based Learning Collaborative Website (www.teambasedlearning. org) to view a list of workshop facilitators.

2. **Advanced Training in TBL** – This workshop is for faculty who have completed basic training in TBL and concentrates on determining what are the fundamental concepts in a course, developing guided learning materials and learning objectives so those concepts can be self-taught, designing student peer evaluation instruments, and establishing in-class strategies for clarifying concepts, thinking through content, and enhancing knowledge, comprehension, and understanding.

3. **Assessing Student Learning** – This includes instruction on how to define course learning outcomes and how to develop instruments that can be used to provide both formative and summative assessments of student learning. Again, there are experts in learning assessment that should be brought in to help faculty to come up with a reasonable number of measurable outcomes. By reasonable, we mean identifying 5 to 10 learning outcomes that when measured indicate that the student is able to apply course knowledge to solve problems or perform a specific clinical task. Dr. Mary Allen, an outstanding expert in the field of learning assessment, frequently conducts assessment workshops for academics in universities throughout the country. She is the author of the book, "Assessing Academic Programs in Higher Education" and has served as a consultant to more than 60 colleges and universities in the United States.

Continuing faculty development is achieved internally by seasoned faculty mentoring less experienced faculty and externally by faculty attending TBL conferences and workshops. As is the case in any pedagogy, it is important to provide faculty routine peer evaluations directed toward continuing improvements in TBL teaching effectiveness. The peer evaluation should critically appraise the organization of a TBL module, the clarity and measurability of learning outcomes, the inter-rater reliability of assessment instruments, the adequacy of the pre-class guided learning materials, appropriateness and quality of readiness assurance test questions, and the significance and relevance of application exercises.

## The Classroom Setting

One of the more interesting details of a TBL course is that it can be taught in a single classroom. Break-out rooms can be used but they are not necessary. In fact, it is easier for the instructor to wander about the classroom and visit each team and not worry about overlooking a team that gathered in a separate room. Your first impression when you enter the classroom is that the noise generated by all the teams will be terribly distracting. But, it isn't. When you stand beside one team in particular you realize that the discussion taking place is occurring with little or no interference from adjacent teams. It is a remarkable phenomenon. It obviously depends on how closely the team members are clustered together, but it surprisingly happens even in a lecture hall. Obviously, a classroom furnished with movable tables and chairs clearly offers an advantage over the lecture hall containing fixed furniture. When the tables and chairs are properly positioned, team members will huddle closely together and, because of the inherent competiveness of the academic arena, they will keep their conversations down to a low volume to prevent other teams from ease-dropping on their analysis, solutions, and discoveries.

## Lessons Learned

Three of the most valuable lessons we have learned in developing an entire curriculum on a TBL frame from scratch relate to increasing individual student accountability, evaluating cumulative knowledge acquisition, and using assessments of critical thinking to design application exercises.

Even though students are involved in evaluating the performance of other students on their respective teams, we have found it necessary to incorporate other strategies for assuring individual accountability in active participation, especially in the conduct of application exercises. Initially, all applications were done by the teams. We referred to these as Team-Based Application Tasks or TBATS. However, it appeared that in some cases some team members were contributing a great deal more in the applications than other team members and that difference was not being documented consistently through student peer evaluations. We therefore initiated Individual-Based

Application Tasks (IBATS). The IBATS were constructed to engage each student individually in the application process, which subsequently leads into a collaborative team approach to reach final consensus on the issues or questions raised in the application exercise. This change increased individual student participation and consequently accountability.

A second lesson we learned is that for some courses it may be necessary to assess cumulative learning. Based on performance and student feedback, we discovered that students struggled with conceptually challenging, high content courses particularly when assessment of understanding was separated 3-6 weeks from application. A modified model of TBL that incorporated regular cumulative assessment tests (ICATS and TCATS) and continuous feedback was adopted for all high content courses. Following the implementation of CATS, performance scores and student feedback demonstrated that the modified model improved the learning occurring from classroom applications to the summative assessments of midterms and finals. The modified TBL model allows for earlier identification and remediation of students who are at risk for falling behind or failing the course. Moreover, our students prefer the modified TBL over the traditional TBL format.

The third lesson was coincidental. We had made a decision to assess the critical thinking skills of our students as they entered our school. We chose a critical thinking assessment test (CAT) that was developed and refined by Dr. Barry Stein and his colleagues at Tennessee Tech University. The CAT assesses a number of critical thinking skills including the following:

1.  Provide alternative explanations for a pattern of evidence that has many possible causes.
2.  Identify additional information needed to evaluate a hypothesis/interpretation.
3.  Provide relevant alternative interpretations of information.
4.  Separate relevant from irrelevant information when searching for information to solve a problem.
5.  Identify alternative suitable solutions for a real-world problem.
6.  Identify and explain the best solution for a real-world problem using relevant information.

When the results of the first CAT our students took were made available to us, we failed to take into account the deficiencies in critical thinking that were identified by the test for making adjustments in our teaching. Then a second class of students took the same CAT and was found to have the same set of deficiencies. After discussing the CAT results for both classes of students we realized that we should utilize the CAT data to design specific application exercises that would help students sharpen their critical thinking skills. Interestingly, two of the critical thinking skills that were shown to be inadequate in both classes are somewhat related – numbers 1 and 5 above. The following two case vignettes are examples of how these two critical thinking skills can be further developed through individual- and team-based application exercises.

**Case 1**: A 52 year-old male patient with a seizure disorder has been placed on 300 mg of phenytoin daily. Despite this usual daily dose, the patient continues to have 1 to 2 seizures every 3 to 4 days. What are three possible explanations for the lack of clinical effectiveness in this patient's anticonvulsant therapy?

**Case 2:** A 62 year-old African-American woman with newly diagnosed hypertension is being managed on 25 mg of hydrochlorothiazide daily. The patient has a history of acute gouty arthritis. She read on WebMD that hydrochlorothiazide can precipitate an acute attack of gout. What alternative medications can be used to manage her hypertension?

These are just three of the important lessons we have learned while developing a TBL pedagogical culture. Many more lessons have been learned and continue to be learned. Motivating faculty to critically appraise what they are learning and make proper changes in the pedagogy closes the assessment loop and also provides a fertile environment for engaging in the scholarship of teaching and learning.